Praise for

EYE OF THE HEART

"*Eye of the Heart* is an immensely original piece of thinking, feeling, writing. There is nothing like it. It opens new terrain, plants new seeds, starts them on their way toward the light."

—ROGER LIPSEY, author of *Gurdjieff Reconsidered*

"By weaving together mystical wisdom, the Fourth Way, and the authority of her own experience, Cynthia Bourgeault masterfully charts a new path of interior transformation through the heart's ability to know and choose the way of love and service. I learned a lot from this book, and I bet you will too."

—CARL MCCOLMAN, author of *The Big Book of Christian Mysticism*

"Reading *Eye of the Heart* is a powerful and clarifying experience. The weaving of personal, metaphysical, and contemporary political insights is amazing, seamless, and intercessory in and of itself. We need this kind of weaving and interpenetrating in our culture just as we need it between the realms."

—TIMOTHY SHRIVER, author of *Fully Alive*

"If ever there was a teacher who could gather the reins of the mind to gallop into the land of the heart (and take us with her), it is Cynthia Bourgeault. This exquisitely written love story distills the intricacies of the esoteric Western traditions into a transformational elixir—both rigorous and luminous—simultaneously intoxicating and sobering. This book is nothing less than a map to the meeting of the worlds at the crossroads of our own souls, one the mapmaker urges us to abandon the minute our heart sees the way."

—MIRABAI STARR, author of *Wild Mercy*

"In *Eye of the Heart* Cynthia Bourgeault invites us on a journey that is profoundly personal and opens us to a truly fresh and panoramic vision of the purpose of human existence. In bringing to our attention the importance of the imaginal realms—the levels of consciousness between our physical reality and our ultimate divine source—she fills an enormous gap in the current conversations on spirituality. Cynthia has an amazing ability to take potentially complex ideas and to explain them with clarity and kindness. Only someone who has actually traversed these realms and knows them well could accomplish such a feat, and she does so with beauty and grace. Any serious student of the Western traditions ought to partake of these teachings. You will be grateful you did!"

—RUSS HUDSON, co-author of *The Wisdom of the Enneagram*

"A brilliant synthesis that both situates the imaginal world and gives it more meaning than it has previously had. . . . [Bourgeault] is a true representative of the Western spiritual tradition."

—from the afterword by A.H. ALMAAS

EYE OF THE HEART

EYE

OF THE

HEART

A Spiritual Journey

into the Imaginal Realm

CYNTHIA BOURGEAULT

with an afterword by A. H. Almaas

SHAMBHALA

Shambhala Publications, Inc.
4720 Walnut Street, Boulder, Colorado 80301
www.shambhala.com

Cover photo: "Sunset Sailboat 1" by Scott Holstein
Cover design: Erin Seaward-Hiatt
Interior design: Claudine Mansour Design
Illustrations: Andrew Breitenberg

9 8 7 6 5 4 3 2 1

First Edition
Printed in the United States of America

♾ This edition is printed on acid-free paper that meets the American
National Standards Institute Z39.48 Standard.
♻ This book is printed on 30% postconsumer recycled paper.
For more information please visit www.shambhala.com.
Shambhala Publications is distributed worldwide by Penguin Random House, Inc.,
and its subsidiaries.

LIBRARY OF CONGRESS CATALOGING-IN-PUBLICATION DATA
Names: Bourgeault, Cynthia, author.
Title: Eye of the heart: a spiritual journey into the imaginal realm /
Cynthia Bourgeault.
Description: First edition. | Boulder, Colorado: Shambhala Publications, Inc., 2020. |
Includes bibliographical references.
Identifiers: LCCN 2019042163 | ISBN 9781611806526 (trade paperback)
Subjects: LCSH: Spirituality. | Spiritual life.
Classification: LCC BL624 .B626 2020 | DDC 204.092 [B]—dc23
LC record available at https://lccn.loc.gov/2019042163

To you, John Kontsas

Despite and because of everything

Here and there does not matter

We must be still and still moving

Into another intensity

For a further union, a deeper communion.

—T. S. ELIOT, "East Coker" (in *The Four Quartets*)

Contents

Preface and Acknowledgments   XI

Prelude: Prospero, Jonah, and "The Greek";
  A Winter's Odyssey   I

One: Introducing the Imaginal   I3

Two: Worlds within Worlds   23

Three: The Great Exchange   43
  Trope: The Hell Realms   63

Four: Imaginal Causality   65

Five: The Art of Shapeshifting   85
  Trope: A School for the Lord's Service   99

Six: Imaginal Purification   I05
  Trope: Putting It All Together   I I9

Seven: What Are We Here For?   I23

Eight: The Conscious Circle of Humanity   139

Nine: Second Body, Abler Soul   157
     Trope: Thomas and Joseph   173

Ten: The Second Rascooarno   179

Afterword by A. H. Almaas   195
Notes   201
Index   213
About the Author   219

Preface and Acknowledgments

THIS BOOK, LONG percolating on the back burner of my mind, was finally torn out of me in the aftermath of a beautiful but brief relationship that left my heart broken wide open to the cosmos. Some of you will shake your heads and say I wrote it simply to process my grief. But if the subject I'm tackling here—the imaginal realm and its mysterious causality—is in fact the chief operative, then it's probably the other way around: the relationship came into my life in order to tease out of me this book. Grief is not the bottom line here, only the alchemical fire. Transfiguration is the bottom line. To John Kontsas, my soulmate for a season, I owe more than I can ever say. You named your boat *Zoi*, Greek for "life," and life is what you gave me—"a good measure, pressed down, shaken together, running over."

Because this book was indeed written substantially in the heat of fusion (in two intense six-week bursts bracketing the summer of 2018), I should perhaps call your attention to a couple of slightly unusual features of its structure, a product of the essentially visionary modality through which it came to be. The book is an exploration of the imaginal realm to be sure, but it is not a scholarly tome. One part spiritual memoir, two parts exegesis, and one part extended prose poem, it is an effort not only to describe that "other intensity" (as T. S. Eliot calls it) but more importantly, to *evoke* it. You will enter the world of this book more comfortably through the gateway of literature than through the gateway of mental speculation. The main part of the work (chapters 1 through 9 exploring various aspects of imaginal reality) is bookended by the story of my own death and transfiguration in the wreckage of a deeply hoped for but ultimately doomed love. And while you can skip over this story and begin at chapter 1, I hope you won't; the depth dimension grows out of the interweaving of the two parts.

The chapters are themselves interwoven with four shorter reflections that I call "tropes." In medieval musicology a trope is a short, lyrical piece attached to a larger element (like a scriptural reading or liturgical text) whose purpose is to comment on and accentuate the larger element, which is exactly how these little tropes are intended to work. They are not fully a part of the chapter they are paired with (and they resisted all efforts to shoehorn them into that format), but in their tangential positioning, they draw out deeper and more "feeling-ful" shades of meaning at work beneath the cognitive surface of the chapters themselves.

I would not have been able to create this book without the luminous support and feedback of Rebecca Parker and Joan Fothergill, my "higher intellectual center" and "higher emotional center," respectively. Both are senior students in my Wisdom network as well as close personal friends. Both are wisely discerning and bottomlessly compassionate. They read each chapter as it emerged from my heart and offered their pristine perspectives in places where I myself could not yet see clearly. Their unfailing confidence that this book was needed in the world right now encouraged me to keep going, even at times when I thought I could not.

I am similarly overwhelmed and deeply moved by the wise and loving support of Roger Lipsey, who read the manuscript from a Gurdjieffian perspective and offered me specifically helpful feedback, together with an unexpectedly comprehensive affirmation, maverick Gurdjieffian that I am. Since Roger is now one of the respected elders in the Gurdjieff Work, I receive his kindness with particular gratitude and hope. We will see how it all unfolds ...

Shambhala Publications has been its usual extraordinary self, though now in a new configuration. When I signed on for this book (and it was actually a different book!), Dave O'Neal was still my managing editor, and we were both very much looking forward to our sixth venture together. Alas, the sword of Damocles descended heavily on my beloved mentor Dave, forcing him into early retirement. But while he was still fighting his way back from a catastrophic stroke that nearly claimed his life, he stepped forward in early January 2019, after I'd sent him an early draft of my manuscript, to champion the new book and argue eloquently for its publication. God love you, Dave! Once again, kindness seems to be the remarkable touchstone here. Where is it coming from?

Sarah Stanton, who now gracefully wears Dave's editorial mantle, has made the mantle her own with a signature clarity, gentleness, and firmness that I already knew a bit about, having worked with her many years ago on my 2004 book *Centering Prayer and Inner Awakening*. The skills I appreciated in her even back then have continued to grow, and her editorial touch with this present book has been a skillful blend of warmth, deep understanding, and clear strategic thinking. The book is stronger for the suggestions she has brought to it, which miraculously do not break its flow but gently widen its inclusivity. I look forward enormously to our continued collaboration if there is indeed yet another book in me.

I also acknowledge with appreciation the steady support of the Shambhala production team including particularly associate editor Audra Figgins, who has "had my back" for three books now, and Lora Zorian, design director, who has been around for even more. Thanks also to copyeditor Jill Rogers, proofreader Amy Chamberlain, and designer Claudine Mansour. And in his usual "tricksy spirit" way, who should suddenly emerge out of nowhere but my gifted Wisdom student Andrew Breitenberg offering his services as the book's graphic designer? Andrew combines a fine illustrator's hand with a deep knowledge of the Wisdom terrain. The results of this inspired collaboration will be appreciated, I am sure, by all.

Finally, I call into my heart with gratitude my wise colleagues who have walked with me through this baptism of fire, contributing not only their professional counsel in some of the painful tight spots but also their loyal and generous presence: Jim Finley, Deborah Jones, Russ Hudson, Jill and Antonio Benet, Buddy Parker, John Moss, and of course my two angels of light, Rebecca and Joan, and my ever-present and all-forgiving archangel, Rafe. Relationships may come and go, but real love—real friendship—abides forever.

—CYNTHIA BOURGEAULT

EYE OF THE HEART

PROSPERO, JONAH, AND "THE GREEK"

A WINTER'S ODYSSEY

Although some illusions are constructions,
not all constructions are illusions.

—EVAN THOMPSON, *Waking, Dreaming, Being*

THE ABOVE MATTER-OF-FACT observation, tucked incon-spicuously into an extended discussion of "Is the Self an Illu-sion?" in the final chapter of Evan Thompson's book *Waking, Dreaming, Being*, wound up rocking my world.[1] So *that* was it, eh? Just because something is a *construction*—a creation of the mind, of the imagination—does not necessarily mean that it is false? There really *is* a Heisenberg dimension to the truth? We really do bushwhack our way toward reality from among a myriad of possible pathways-over-the-ground by the one we choose to activate?

"Hermeneutics is always a wager," my teacher Rafe had told me shortly before his death. "A wager that if your premises are right, you'll live it into action."

Rafe—a.k.a. Brother Raphael Robin—was the hermit monk of St. Benedict's Monastery in Snowmass, Colorado. He lived in a small cabin about a mile above the monastery from which he emerged periodically to fulfill his duties as monastic handyman, then returned as quickly as possible to resume his lonely vigil at the edge of the cosmic vastness. I met him accidentally while attending a Centering Prayer retreat and instantly recognized him as "the real deal." He seemed to embody the combination I had been intuitively searching for all my life: a deeply attuned mystical heart anchored in a fierce conscious presence. "When the student is ready, the teacher appears," as the old adage goes, and we both knew, essentially from that first meeting, that our lives from then on were destined to be profoundly intertwined.

Within a matter of months I had closed out my operations in Maine and moved to Snowmass to work full-time with him. For the remaining two-and-a-half years of his human life we were pretty much inseparable, teacher and student and human beloveds in equal measure. Our work together was grounded not only in our mutual love for the Christian mystical tradition but also in our mutual admiration for G. I. Gurdjieff, the early-twentieth-century Armenian-born spiritual master whose teachings seemed to offer a practical access route to the transformative power coiled within that tradition. I had studied the Gurdjieff Work (as this teaching is known by its devotees) formally in groups; Rafe had devoured it in books alone up at his cabin. When we began to put our respective puzzle pieces together, the sparks flew in all directions, both figuratively and literally.

After Rafe's death in December 1995, I did indeed take him up on his hermeneutical wager. In no doubt the biggest spiritual gamble of my life, I went back to those same puzzle pieces and out of them constructed an elaborate metaphysical castle to account for my raw sense that our connection was still fully intact. The major building blocks of this construction were the stipulation of an "abler soul" between us—a subtle energetic vehicle for continued growth and exchange beyond the grave—plus the intimation of an ongoing spiritual partnership in "the conscious circle of humanity" as we journeyed together to the completion of our respective earthly and heavenly tasks. This latter notion (again Gurdjieffian in origin) had grabbed Rafe particularly in our many conversations on the subject before his death. He understood it as a sphere of active collaboration between the realms in which advanced souls still in their human bodies and others now living in the realms beyond join hands across the life/death divide to create a single living stream of compassion and wisdom to literally encircle our planet and help steady its course. Rafe yearned to belong to that circle, and in saying yes to the wager that he did in fact make it there, I implicitly offered myself as the hands on this side that would join his in an ongoing conscious partnership for the rest of my human life and perhaps well beyond it. That vision would set my compass heading for the next quarter of a century.

It was, admittedly, a pretty high-stakes gamble, undertaken at least in part to hold back the walls of despair and keep walking toward the vision that in our brief human time together we had so powerfully shared. But it was, in the final analysis, a construction, and I knew it. Perhaps indeed a "concocted fantasy," as an offended acquaintance in my wider circle of monastery friends dubbed it. Other explanations were close at hand and way more psychologically obvious: I was delusional, for starters—so needy that I would throw Rafe's good and worthy spiritual reputation into the breach in order to secure my own self-validation. "I would have loved to hear Rafe's side of the story," one reviewer of my book *Love Is Stronger Than Death* (where I laid all this out), commented dryly.

I knew she had me there. Rafe wasn't going to speak, at least not in any way that this reviewer or most anyone else would recognize. Along the way, over the years, a few of my friends would swear that they, too, felt his presence. But they were mostly drawn from the ranks of my closest and most psychically attuned supporters, so it was hard to eliminate the suggestibility factor. From those who might be counted as more credible witnesses—Rafe's former monastic brethren, for example—I heard nothing. There were no visitations, no parallel Rafe sightings to suggest that he was alive and working anywhere else than in my overwrought imagination.

But the fruits were good. That was the one piece of countervailing evidence. On the strength of this so-called concocted fantasy, I slowly began to move forward into my life. The doors opened, and the teaching began to flow, a dynamic alchemy of all those amazing insights that Rafe and I had experimented with and had mutually drawn forth in our brief time together. Little by little this still-nascent wisdom lineage began to distinguish itself from among the general haze of contemplative Christianities, interior monasticisms, and other initiatives that started to roll out into the new century. Even Rafe's former monastic brethren at Snowmass, while denying any specific Rafe epiphanies, reported back that my own transformation was evident and growing. I was psychologically strong and spiritually clear. *Something* was obviously working.

And my sense of connection with Rafe held steady from within. Construction or illusion, the two of us were birthing a Wisdom lineage whose influence was beginning to make itself felt as an actual energetic nexus. And while I felt (and still do) like the cabin boy steering the schooner, somehow, with Rafe there on the other side and me watching my p's and q's carefully, we managed to keep the ship on course.

Somewhere during the more recent years, I began to notice our internal positioning shifting ever so slightly. From my end it felt like a widening space between us as the scope of Rafe's "majesty" (Jacob Boehme's term meaning cosmic agency and responsibility) began to increase noticeably. And this was to be expected, after all. "Rafe" was short for Raphael, the monastic name bestowed upon him when he entered the novitiate, and it was toward the archangelic realm that he was now clearly gravitating. On my end of the tether, this shift expressed itself outwardly as a new emphasis on the prophetic, evolutionary, and collective. In 2015 I received a powerful cosmic nudge to dive into the work of Jesuit scientist and mystic Pierre Teilhard de Chardin, and so I did. My understanding of contemplative transformation became more evolutionary, more drawn to models expressing this new vision of collective responsibility. As the political situation in the world grew daily more dicey, I began to sense our Wisdom school being called to a very specific post, a very specific imaginal and vibrational task. We seemed to be charged with weaving together some very important dialogical threads (between Gurdjieff and Teilhard, for example), and with joining our work with other schools at a similar vibrational level in order to help hold a collective energy field sorely needed on a planet about to undergo a major contraction. On November 7, 2016, the eve of the American election that launched the world into the Trump era, I received a very explicit directive in this regard at Tintern Abbey, the sacked Cistercian monastery of Wordsworthian fame, and the reconstitution of our lineage as a conscious circle of humanity began in earnest. It was rich, purposeful, blessed work, and I felt honored to be holding up my end of the stick.

On the inside, I guess I was lonely—or maybe just growing, too, in continuing sync with Rafe. His widening space certainly left a hole in a heart that had never fully healed from his first departure, and all those years of living cheek-to-jowl with the painful specter of self-delusion had gradually taken their toll. Or maybe again, consistent with that "wager" hermeneutic, I was simply becoming more and more restless living out my days in a Prospero's castle (to draw on the metaphor so powerfully portrayed in Shakespeare's mysteriously soul-riveting final play, *The Tempest*). I found myself wondering more and more whether this had all been simply an elaborate mental *son et lumière*, to be dispelled by a single flick of the magician's wand accompanied by the solemn utterance, "All . . . shall dissolve, and, like this insubstantial pageant faded, leave not one rack behind."[2] My growing scent for a more direct perception kind of truth was increasingly beckoning me to step out of the nest and see what, if anything, actually held me up. Not because I doubted Rafe, but because I trusted the direction in which he invariably pointed: straight into the unknown. And because one of the final pieces of wisdom he had left me with was, "When the building's completed, you no longer need the scaffolding."

"It's Johnny!"

All of these currents were swirling around in the background in the summer of 2017 as I found myself drifting more and more into the gravitational field of fellow wharf rat and local badass hero, Johnny "The Greek" Kontsas. I'd always cherished my summer downtime to play with my boats and take a breather from spiritual earnestness by hanging out with the Stonington fishing crowd. Johnny was clearly the pied piper among them. With his distinctive Brooklyn/Boston nasal twang and his Marlboro Man patina (complete with hand-rolled cigarette dangling from the corner of his mouth most the day), he was a striking presence around Stonington harbor, meting out mischief and merriment in equal measure.

As our initial barbed repartee gradually gave way to occasional shafts of deep sharing, I could see more and more what a rare character he was. Rough edged but intuitively brilliant ("I'm an old soul," he claimed), he was a consummate water man, a free thinker, and an unquenchable dreamer. A few seasons back he'd pooled his resources to buy a thirty-seven-foot catamaran, which he named *Zoi*, Greek for "life force." He lived aboard her in Stonington harbor during the summer, earning his living as a diver and marine-related jack-of-all-trades. Come the first cold winds of fall, he'd depart for seven months of singlehanded cruising in the Caribbean. Fiercely present, agile as a cat, and unyielding as Diogenes in his pursuit of truth, he was a one-man countercultural statement.

During the fall, we gradually entwined hearts. He was skeptical at first, I the more insistent. By now, in my imaginative free flight he was fully my watery Shams Tabrizi, and I yearned for both the initiation and the intimacy, I guess in equal parts.

I'm not sure what he yearned for. "Joyful companionship," he acknowledged—perhaps against all odds, his still-elusive soulmate. We were a pretty odd-duck couple, but we also had a lot going for us. Both of us loved the water, shared a similar spirit of adventure, and were ostensibly free and available for a new relationship. By late fall we were also deeply taken with each other. We decided to give it a go. I bid farewell to my seafaring Shams as he departed Stonington harbor in early November, then joined him in Florida four weeks later to hoist sail for the Caribbean.

We made it for five weeks before that first round collapsed.

Almost immediately, things started to go wrong. There were the usual adjustments facing two persons of very different backgrounds and temperaments suddenly thrust into close quarters on one person's turf. All garden variety relational stuff, and we soldiered through it bravely, buoyed up by interludes of almost unbearable sweetness. But there were also some deeper pathologies that began to surface, presaging a much more ominous San Andreas Fault running through this happy country of the heart.

Then the accidents started to happen. The radar fell down and washed overboard one night for no apparent reason, leaving us with only the moon (fortunately coming on full) to navigate by. The anchor compartment flooded, knocking out the winch that ran the windlass (John rebuilt it from scratch, gifted mechanic that he is), and later an engine compartment flooded (busted hose). The water pump, alternator, and starter were all damaged in the flood—John rebuilt them as well. We were beset by headwinds almost the whole trip, and by the time we reached the Windward Islands on round 2, those winds were blowing gale force—and remained so, right on our nose, for nine days straight. We sailed on undaunted, the captain supremely in command of his ship, but poor *Zoi* took quite a beating. The starboard stay frayed (John sistered it with a nylon line), the sails tore (John patched them), and the auto-helm cracked (John lashed and epoxied it back together).

What was going on here? When Johnny put the question to two of his old seafaring buddies, they instantly offered the same response: "You've got a Jonah onboard."

We laughed—a tad nervously, at first. Who wants their cruising dreams held hostage by an old Biblical shillelagh? But this *did* seem like a rather extraordinary string of bad luck. And the assaults got worse. On the next-to-the-last day of round 2, I stupidly caught my left leg in a moving coil of rope while releasing a dock line and fractured my ankle. Two days later John got food poisoning from some bad chicken he'd bought after dropping me off in Antigua and was sick for nearly the entire month I was gone.

Then, in probably the most whirlwind disintegration I have

ever experienced, we both watched in horror as that San Andreas Fault erupted full force less than a week into our round 3, turning what had begun as a joyful birthday celebration and beginning exploration of a more permanent commitment into a devastating wreckage of our hearts and our dreams.

I'm still not sure why.

There any number psychological explanations, of course. Some favor me, some favor the Greek. Let's just leave it that the components of this psychic stew were anger, clinging, distrust, and most likely an underlying borderline pattern where love turns lightning fast to demonization. But were those the actual *causes* of the unraveling, or merely the stress cracks along which the fracturing ran its course?

Safely back in Maine, I reread the Jonah story, then reread it again and yet again. Folktale that it may be, I had to admit that the whole picture was finally starting to make sense. All it took was a single flip of the switch, from the presumption that I was a free agent to an acceptance of the premise that my two-decade imaginal partnership with Rafe was a construction, not an illusion. Then all the pieces of the puzzle began to fall into place.

Note to self: Jonah was a *prophet,* remember? He held an imaginal post, a post in that realm connecting divine will to its actualization here on earth. The whole saga began when God announced to Jonah that he was to be deployed to Nineveh in order to read the riot act to the city's wayward residents. Jonah didn't much relish the assignment and decided to take an unannounced leave of absence. He found a ship bound for Tarshish and a captain willing to take him there. He embarked, no doubt pleased with himself for having given God the slip. Then all hell broke loose.

Was I that prophet gone AWOL?

If this world were the only world that's *real* (the interior realms being purely subjective), then I was indeed free and clear to give my heart to the Greek. I told him I was free and clear. I really believed it. And so did he—almost. It was that "almost" that tore our love apart.

In the end, when all other courses of action had been exhausted, there was nothing for Jonah to do but admit defeat. He had been cosmically checkmated, and he knew it. Turning to his captain, he said, "Pick me up and throw me into the sea, that it may quiet down for you: for I know that it is because of me that this violent storm has come upon you" (Jon. 1:12).

For my birthday a couple of weeks earlier Johnny had gotten me my first wetsuit. He'd long been wanting to share this special part of his life with me, and on the morning of that final long day's journey into night, we decided to give it a go. I wriggled into the suit, laughing at the word "deep" emblazoned on the chest. "My students will love this!" I joked. I donned the facemask and air hose he'd hooked up and made my first dive into the sparkling azure sea. So entranced were we by the whole unfolding that at the time neither of us quite registered that the logo I was actually wearing on my chest was not "deep." Beneath the word there was also a number.

The number 6.

You gotta hand it to imaginal synchronicity.

Jonah himself would be *physically* deep-sixed, tossed overboard by a reluctant captain, to find his place of reckoning in the belly of the whale. On the whole, I fared a lot better. Over the next twenty-four hours most of the totems of our budding love would go overboard in a tumultuous ritual divesting: birthday cards, valentines, gifts, my Christmas bicycle and guitar—and yes, my red hat, for fifteen years the symbol of my imaginal post, which vanished somewhere during the night. A more pointed cosmic message I cannot imagine.

But I myself did not go overboard. And my belly of the whale became instead a small, dark hotel room dockside in Nassau where John dropped me hastily at first light on Maundy Thursday before heading straight back out to sea.

I trust it has now quietened down for you, dear captain of my heart.

The Belly of the Whale

When all is said and done, the Jonah story still seems like the simplest and kindest explanation. Johnny and I were cosmically checkmated. Even after factoring in all the psychological stuff, there's still that additional X factor, which looks suspiciously like a higher hand at work. There are simply too many highly configured "coincidences" (they're actually called chiasms) to chalk it up to a mere string of bad luck. Once you've learned the language of imaginal causality, it reads like an open book. The bottom line is *no*. The subtext is *"Disregard at your own peril."* We escaped with our lives this time. Another time we might not be so lucky.

Was this cosmic "cease and desist" order issued for dereliction of duty, for our own protection, or to force us to find a whole new basis for relationship? I am not yet able to say; the work of sorting through the wreckage has only just begun. But if, as philosopher Karl Popper famously asserted, "Truth arises more swiftly out of error than out of confusion," then that winter's testing of the waters had certainly been a quantum leap toward a more truthful place. It's ironic that the "proof positive" of my imaginal calling, which I could never quite find my way to from the inside, should be delivered so forcefully from the outside through a stern cosmic reprimand. But confirmation is confirmation in whatever form it arrives, and at least I now know where my own work of inner accounting must begin.

Not all constructions are illusions—so true, so true. A Prospero's castle this imaginal journey with Rafe may be—yes, even a "concocted fantasy"—but over the years it has weathered the gales of truth-testing and time-and-again proved itself real. Maybe, as in that old children's story *The Velveteen Rabbit*, "real" is not where you start out but where you wind up; you become real gradually when somebody loves you for a long, long time. However Rafe and I managed to arrive here—through whatever random combination of truth seeking, risk taking, and fidelity to each other and to the path—this imaginal partnership has become my home, my spiritual workplace, and my post. Good work has been done here, and I am still apparently needed. Prospero's castle it may be, but the castle is built over a springhead, and there is water in the well.

But as I pick up my water bucket and resume course for Nineveh, it is not without a long backward glance toward a small catamaran plying its solitary way toward open sea. I know what I must do for now. I must write. And you, Greek, must sail. That is the way it is.

One

INTRODUCING
THE IMAGINAL

SO WHERE DO I begin to tell the story? How to introduce you
to my neighborhood? It is all too easy when exploring topics
as inherently elusive as the imaginal to hide out in mental
maneuvers. Is the imaginal the same as the Platonic "intelli-
gible universe?" The Hindu subtle levels of consciousness, or
the bardo realms of Tibetan Buddhism? Maybe yes, maybe no,
but in any case that's not what I'm about here. If there's one
thing I've learned from these two-and-a-half decades of imaginal bushwhacking, it's that the imaginal realm is entered only
through the heart. How you get there is where you'll arrive.
And so by whatever route our exploration leads us, it will need
to stay close to the heart.

Fortunately, that is not really so difficult with the imaginal
realm, for the heart really is its native ground. And when all
the intellectual abstractions have been stripped away, and it
is allowed to speak in its own native tongue, what it speaks of,
with surprising simplicity and directness, is beauty, hope, and
a mysteriously deeper order of coherence and aliveness flowing through this earthly terrain connecting it to the infinite
wellsprings of cosmic creativity and abundance. Instead of the
isolation and anomie so often conveyed in our postmodern
cosmological roadmaps (where we are simply an insignificant

planet in an insignificant galaxy in a random "big bang" among a ceaseless cacophony of big bangs), it speaks of the preciousness of our human particularity and the exigency of our human contribution (tiny though it may be) to that vast, dynamic web of cosmic interbeing, which can be seen, in toto, as the heart of God. It calls us to a renewed sense of dignity, accountability, belongingness, cosmic intimacy, and love. That is why I am writing this book, and for no other reason. Our hearts get this language already. With only a bit of a shove—and perhaps a slightly new roadmap—our heads may be able to get it too. Pray to God, while there is still time.

So perhaps "where to begin" in a more heartful way might be with that striking image furnished by Jesus himself: "In my Father's house are many mansions." Picture the imaginal realm as one such mansion, belonging mostly to the Western spiritual tradition and deeply related to the Western experience of the heart of God. It is perhaps not a high mansion and certainly not a universal one (since many spiritual traditions seem to get on perfectly well without it). But within its own domain, i.e., the Western mystical and esoteric tradition, it is a pivotal one. Something important happens here.

Please don't think of it as a *place.* I know it's nearly impossible for the Western mind not to go there. We did the same thing with heaven and hell, didn't we? Turned them into miniature planets, complete with fiery furnaces or pearly gates. But a realm is not fundamentally a place; it is more like a set of governing conventions that make possible a certain kind of manifestation. In our own earth realm we are subject to many such governing conventions (we call them "laws"). Gravity holds our feet to the ground. Time flows in one direction only. We cannot walk through walls, be in two places at once, or wish ourselves ten pounds lighter. There are a lot of laws (forty-eight of them, Gurdjieff postulated), making our earth plane a fairly dense and determinate place. There are other realms that are lighter and a few that are denser. We will meet some of these in due course. For now it's important to keep reminding ourselves that from a metaphysical perspective, realm has less to do with physical location than with density. In fact, virtually all spiritual teachers in all traditions have insisted that the "higher" (i.e., less dense) realms are not somewhere else but *within*—already coiled inside us as subtler and yet more intensely alive bandwidths of experience and perception. The reason we do not typically notice them is that the laws governing any realm are generally too coarse to allow the penetration of those finer vibrations emanating from the next realm "up" into its normal sphere of operations. As St. Paul reminds us, we do indeed "see through a glass darkly."

But why do we call it "imaginal?" I admit that the whole issue is problematic. The term itself has its immediate provenance in Islamic mysticism, where it denotes a subtle and fluid "intermediate" realm suspended midway between form and formlessness. But the idea itself—or archetype, actually—is a mainstay of the Western tradition of *sophia perennis*, or "perennial wisdom," with roots going all the way back to Plato.[1] Within this wider tradition it is typically understood to be a boundary zone separating the denser causality of our earth plane from the finer causalities that lie "above" us in the angelic and logoic worlds. Put more simply, it sits on the dividing line between the visible and invisible worlds—or, according to the older, pre-Einsteinian metaphysics, between the "spiritual" and "material" worlds.

It is called "imaginal" because, while it is invisible to the physical eye, it is still clearly perceptible through the eye of the heart, which is in fact what the word *imagination* specifically implies in its original Islamic context: *direct perception through the eye of the heart, not through mental reflection or fantasy.* Of course, in the modern West we now view the interior landscape through the filter of Wordsworthian romanticism and hear the word *imagination* as suggesting something personal, subjective, illusory, or "made up"—which is of course exactly the opposite of what the term is actually intended to convey.

I know this causes a lot of unnecessary confusion, but once you get used to the real metaphysical meaning of the term, it sheds a lot of light not only on the Islamic mystical tradition but on the Christian mystical tradition as well. I am quite certain, for example, that this direct noetic seeing is what St. Paul had in mind by the term *faith* (as in "faith is the substance of things hoped for, the evidence of things not seen"). But in our own diminished age even faith has now gone dark and tends to be understood as a "blind" leap into the dark rather than a luminous perception of the invisible golden thread. Small wonder that the imaginal has all but dropped off the contemporary metaphysical roadmap.

I spoke of the imaginal realm a few paragraphs ago as a "boundary realm," but it is actually more of a confluence, for the word *boundary* suggests a separation while what is really at stake in this realm is an active flowing together. "Where the two seas meet" is a beautiful Sufi metaphor to convey the essence of what actually goes on here. The imaginal is a meeting ground, a kind of cosmic intertidal zone—and as in all intertidal zones, nourishment and metamorphosis furnish the principal order of business here. In this realm the fruits of our human striving—both conscious and unconscious—are offered up to the whole. From this realm, in turn, we receive blessing, inspiration, guidance, and vivifying force, which are ours to share and bestow here below. Like a Sufi dervish, we receive and bestow, receive and bestow, as we turn and are turned within the greater cosmic dance.

In its traditional metaphysical positioning this connective

work of the imaginal realm does not come immediately to the fore because of the strong underlying metaphysical bias toward "substance ontology," i.e., the assumption that matter and spirit are qualitatively different items, distinct and fundamentally irreconcilable in nature. Viewed through this lens, the imaginal and "material" realms perch on either side of a fundamental ontological divide—or as they say here in Maine, "You can't get there from here." But in a post-Einsteinian era it is no longer possible to think that way; the old metaphysical maps must be redrawn to a new baseline in which *energy*, not substance, is the coin of the realm.

Esotericist Valentin Tomberg is thinking along these lines in his *Meditations on the Tarot* when he invites us to reimagine the Great Chain of Being as a single energetic continuum:

> Modern science has come to understand that matter is only condensed energy.... Sooner or later science will discover that what it calls "energy" is only condensed psychic force—which discovery will lead in the end to the establishment of the fact that psychic force is the "condensation," pure and simple, of consciousness, i.e., spirit.[2]

"Psychic force" here refers to the subtler energies that science does not yet know how to measure but that have demonstrable effect in the physical world—for example, the energies of attention, will, prayer, and love. It is the transmission of these energies that furnishes the supreme business of the imaginal world. In this updated and much more dynamic revisioning, the imaginal can be roughly situated at the junction between the "psychic energy" and "physical energy" bandwidths, where its pivotal positioning in the transmission chain comes much more into focus.

At the risk of overloading the circuits in this very preliminary introduction, I would add that the Jesuit mystic and scientist Pierre Teilhard de Chardin is describing essentially these same two energetic bandwidths with his terms *radial energy* and *tangential energy*.[3] The latter is the physical energy that keeps our world chugging along on its axis; the former is the finer and more purposeful energy that draws the world forward toward its evolutionary destiny. Radial energy is released and generated specifically through the interplay with tangential energy, and it is for Teilhard explicitly *counterentropic*. This is a very good point to remember, even at this early stage.

Impressionistically, the imaginal penetrates this denser world in much the same way as the fragrance of perfume penetrates an entire room, subtly enlivening and harmonizing. My favorite image to begin to access this admittedly mind-bending notion still comes by way of a striking vignette in Isak Dinesen's *Out of Africa,* in which she recounts how she once came upon a beautiful snake moving through the grass, its skin glistening with subtle, variegated colors. She raved so much about that snakeskin that one of her house servants killed the snake, skinned it, and made it into a belt for her. But to her dismay, the once glistening skin was now merely dull and gray, because all along the beauty had lain not in the physical skin, but in the quality of the aliveness. The imaginal is that quality of aliveness moving through this realm, interpenetrating, cohering, filling things with the fragrance of implicit meaning whose lines do not converge in this world alone but at a point beyond. As the Gospel of Thomas describes it:

> I am the light shining upon all things,
> I am the sum of everything, for from me
> Everything has come, and toward me
> Everything returns. Pick up a stone and there I am,
> Split a piece of wood and you will find me there.[4]

Experientially, received within one's own quiet subjectivity, it appears as an allusive aliveness, a meaning presenting itself in "glimpses and visions," a foretaste—or aftertaste—of a reality half-forgotten but still strangely familiar, of an intensity and beauty and coherence that seems to match the actual pattern of our hearts if only we could stand to live there.

Is It Real?

I cannot emphasize strongly enough that the word *imaginal* does not mean "imaginary." That unfortunate but all-too-understandable confusion was created by Henry Corbin, the noted Islamic scholar, when he introduced the term *mundus imaginalis* to name that intermediate, invisible realm of causality that figures so prominently in mystical Islamic cosmology. But in so doing, Corbin was drawing on a highly technical and quintessentially Islamic notion of imagination as itself being one of those higher and more subtle energies, possessing will, objectivity, and creative agency. To our modern Western ears, the word *imaginal* may indeed seem to suggest some private or subjective inner landscape, "make believe" or fanciful by nature. But while it is typically associated with the world of dreams, visions, and prophecy, i.e., a more subtle form, the imaginal is always understood within traditional metaphysics to be *objectively real* and in fact comprising "an ontological reality entirely superior to that of mere possibility."[5] It designates a sphere that is not less real but *more real* than our so-called "objective reality" and whose generative energy can (and does) change the course of events in this world. Small though it may appear to be, it is mighty, as those who try to swim against it will readily attest.

Walter Wink, one of the few contemporary mainstream Christian theologians who have been bold enough to venture appreciatively into the terrain of the imaginal, describes how this "generative" causality played out in the events following the resurrection. His comments below offer a clear window into both of these key points: imaginal reality is "objective," and it carries real force:

> It is a prejudice of modern thought that events happen only in the outer world. What Christians regard as the most significant event in human history happened, according to the gospels, in the psychic realm, and it altered external history irrevocably. Ascension was an "objective" event, if you will, but it took place in the imaginal realm, at the substratum of human existence where the most fundamental changes in consciousness take place. The ascension was a "fact" on the imaginal plane, not just an assertion of faith. It irreversibly altered the nature of the disciples' consciousness.[6]

One need only to read the Book of Acts to sense the breadth and power of this change in the disciples' consciousness and to grasp the implications of what Wink is saying here. It is true that not all constructions are illusions. However and wherever these disciples came to it, they emerged from the post-resurrection events infused with a clear and high sense of purpose, resolve, empowerment, and above all, the unshakable confidence that their Lord was still present with them—which at the imaginal level is undisputedly true. With their oars planted firmly in that kingdom, they moved forward to change the world. This is exactly what Corbin was trying to convey by the word *imagination*, understood in the traditional sense. Imaginal reality is a valid construction which, by changing consciousness in its inner ground, changes the nature of reality in the outer world.

And of course, from the opposite end of the spectrum, that's exactly the headwind that Johnny and I were encountering in our Jonah syndrome: the imaginal realm as causal, purposive, and fiercely determined in regard to this one. From the outside it made no sense whatsoever why two adventurous and ostensibly available people should not be able to escape together for a winter's odyssey in the Caribbean. But the force of the interrealmic disharmony shook the sails and toppled the radar. The message was loud and clear.

Because of this demonstrated capacity to affect outcome in this world, the imaginal realm has long been associated with the world of prophecy and oracles. To attuned hearts, it does indeed seem to send "messages," as it surely did for the disciples, for Jonah, and for Johnny and me. That is why it often is equated with the "subtle" level of consciousness in contemporary roadmaps such as those promulgated by philosopher Ken Wilber.[7] There is truth here, to be sure, but remember that these "levels of consciousness" maps are all essentially "upper left quadrant" metaphysics, to use Wilberspeak—or in other words, geared to the individual interior journey and individual transformation. Properly understood through its own Western filter, the imaginal realm is *collective and evolutionary*; its ultimate purpose is to guide, shape, nourish, and, where necessary, offer course corrections to our entire planetary and interplanetary unfolding. As an objectively verifiable realm interpenetrating our earth plane and operating at a twice-higher frequency of spiritual intensity and coherence, it is a life within a life, and its laws, interpenetrating our own, provide the inner template by which the outer unfolding can proceed rightly.

Therefore, it is also and primarily supremely the realm of *cosmic assistance*. It is the "place" from which saints, teachers, masters, and all manner of abler souls reach out across the apparent divide between the worlds to support or where necessary modify earthly outcomes in tandem with willing and attuned hearts here below.

And that point, perhaps underemphasized in the traditional roadmaps, turns out to be the linchpin.

Two

WORLDS WITHIN WORLDS

OUR OWN EARTH realm has long been known on the cosmological maps as *mixtus orbis*, the "mixed realm." While the full explanation for this designation is complex, something does seem to get mixed and mingled here. We humans are curiously bilingual; we speak the language of this world with all its charms and nuances, but we also strain toward that invisible other that seems to hover right beyond us in those dazzling glimpses and visions: that intuition of "another intensity," in the words of T. S. Eliot, to which we know we also belong. [1] That invisible but always interpenetrating other is the imaginal realm.

The earlier metaphysical roadmaps, as mentioned, tended to draw a sharp dividing line between matter and spirit, with the result that the imaginal, hovering just on the horizon of our *mixtus orbis*, often appeared to be a world in itself, with no obvious commerce with our own. As the last outpost of the "spiritual" realms, how and why would it bridge the divide into the material realms? In the previous chapter I tried to recast this traditional metaphysical habit in terms of the more contemporary understanding that there is in fact no such "divide" but rather a single continuum of energy manifesting in various degrees of subtlety or coarseness. Transposing the metaphysical map from its original Platonic milieu to this more Einsteinian one in fact takes us far beyond traditional esoteric understandings of the imaginal, which focused on the personal and elusive nature of this realm, into a new appreciation of its collective and evolutionary importance.

It was Gurdjieff who really got the ball rolling here by adding in the key puzzle piece (undetectable through the lens of traditional sophia perennis metaphysics), which he called "reciprocal feeding." He proposed that along the entire Ray of Creation (his equivalent term for the Great Chain of Being), there is a continuous, active exchange proceeding in *both* directions—not only from higher realms to lower but also from lower to higher—in order to maintain the entire ray in a state of dynamic equilibrium according to a cosmic principle to which he gives the rather unwieldy name "Trogoautoegocrat." Mouthful though the term may be, the idea itself is a remarkably prescient attempt to view the entire created order as what we would nowadays call a "self-specifying system," a whole greater than the sum of its parts, whose chief metaphysical feature is no longer *involution*—the gradual loss of energy as the lower end of the chain plunges steadily toward entropy—but rather an elaborate homeostasis that preserves (and even increases) the energy of the total system as each realm makes its required contribution to the whole.

Gurdjieff referred to this system as "reciprocal *feeding*" for good reason: the exchange he has in mind involves the actual transformation of cosmic substances—more like digestion than the simple information-sharing favored in contemporary consciousness-based models. The full articulation of this idea leads us swiftly into one of the densest jungles of Gurdjieffian arcana: his notorious "hydrogen tables," a maze of esoteric chemistry in which many an overly cerebral seeker has lost the plot.[2] But the idea itself is fairly straightforward and so flagrantly timely for a planet careening toward ecological catastrophe that I believe it's simply no longer conscionable to allow it to be held captive in a maze of Gurdjieffian Fourth Way esoterica. More to our immediate concern here, this broader vision of what amounts to a vast intergalactic bootstrapping is utterly essential if we hope to have some true feeling for what the imaginal realm is all about, beyond just some allusive bandwidth of inner guidance and bedazzling intensity. If exchange is indeed the principal business of this realm, we must picture this exchange from the outset as a two-way street.

What I would like to attempt in this chapter, then, is to offer a nontechnical version of reciprocal feeding, shorn of its quasi-chemical nomenclature but still conveying the gist of Gurdjieff's most brilliant ecological intuition. This will set the cosmological backdrop for a closer and more substantive look at what the imaginal realm contributes to this operation—and more to the point, what *we* contribute to what the imaginal contributes to this operation.

I should make clear from the outset that what I am about to lay before you is *not* "Gurdjieff 101." Gurdjieff does not even actually use the term "imaginal" in his teaching (although he clearly drank from these same mystical Islamic wells),[3] so the synthesis here is my own, culled not only from the Gurdjieff teaching but from what I've learned from Rafe, my own inner work, and the greater Christian mystical tradition particularly as seen through the eyes of my two most reliable guides, Jacob Boehme and Pierre Teilhard de Chardin. You might think of it more as my own cosmological reflection, glimpsed while standing on the shoulders of these three visionary geniuses (four counting Rafe), whom I believe are all fundamentally looking in the same direction.

The Ray of Creation

Gurdjieff actually makes use of *two* cosmic maps, and to situate the imaginal sphere of operations within his teaching, you have to overlay them.

The first, and probably more widely known of these (because of its close tie-in with the enneagram and the Law of Seven), is his Ray of Creation, which, as I have mentioned already, is the Gurdjieffian version of the Great Chain of Being. In most respects this follows the standard processionary model of traditional sophia perennis metaphysics, with progressively denser and colder kingdoms emerging out of that initial fiery explosion of the divine will-to-form that sets the whole thing in motion. The counterentropic trajectory is not at first clearly visible.

What is immediately interesting about this map, however, is that the entire ray is located within the *physical* universe—although of course, the word *physical* here must be expanded to the widest and wildest reaches of our cosmological imagination. Gurdjieff's "Megalocosmos," the vast celestial canvas on which his map is drawn, stretches even beyond the fourteen billion years of our present "universe story," reaching back into that implicitly endless matrix from which big bangs emerge like virtual particles. It is on the grandest possible cosmic scale that his vision plays out.

So too, the realms on this ray are not named by spiritual or theological names, as is typical of sophia perennis metaphysics. You will not find here logoic realms, angelic realms, heaven and hell realms—or for that matter, imaginal realms. Instead, you will find actual interplanetary locations, named in an order that some of you may find strangely familiar: *dominus* (Holy Absolute), *siderum* (all galaxies), *lactera* (Milky Way, our galaxy), *sol* (our sun), *fatum* (fate, our own solar system or sphere of planetary influence), *mixtus orbis* ("mixed realm," our planet earth), *regina coeli* (queen of the heavens, the moon)—or *do, si,⁴ la, sol, fa, mi, re, do.*

Wait a minute! Isn't that our modern Western musical scale?

Indeed, it is. And this is where the second fascinating feature of the Ray of Creation comes in. According to Gurdjieff, our modern major scale actually preserves in the names of its notes and the arrangement of its intervals a vestigial memory of an ancient esoteric teaching about the "cosmic solfeggio" (as contemporary Gurdjieff commentator James Moore wittily dubs it), not only in the way in which the created order originally came into existence but also in the way in which *energy is continuously transmitted and replenished along the Ray of Creation.* That knowledge is still there, hidden in plain sight in the musical scale, to be dug out by those so inclined; its articulation dovetails precisely with what in the Gurdjieff Work is known as the Law of Seven, the Law of World Maintenance.

This is not the place to get sidetracked into a lengthy discussion of the Law of Seven. Those of you who wish to can read more about it in my book *The Holy Trinity and the Law of Three* as well as in any number of Gurdjieffian textbooks.⁵ But from the point of view of imaginal exchange, it does yield up one very interesting piece of data, again a stable feature of the Law of Seven. If you look at the schematic that follows, you notice those two lines cutting across the map, between *do* and *si* near the top and between *fa* and *mi* closer to the bottom. These correspond to the "hesitation" points on the ray—half steps on the musical scale—where a new infusion of energy, or a different *kind* of energy, must be introduced in order to keep the whole ray flowing on trajectory. Otherwise the whole thing will veer off track or be halted at a threshold it cannot cross. In Gurdjieffian terminologies, these are the "shock" points, the places where the entire progression is the most vulnerable but, equally, the most permeable.

In the case of the higher (*do-si*) shock point, that bridging energy is provided by the will of the Holy Absolute, still close enough to ground zero to easily span the descending gap. In the latter case, as we will see shortly, the shock point falls right between *fa*, the traditional endpoint of the so-called subtle realms, and *mi*, the beginning of those "dense material realms." And this is exactly the place where traditional metaphysics and I (see my discussion of Gurdjieff's second map, following shortly) locate the imaginal realm. In other words, the *mi-fa* shock point falls right in the middle of the imaginal intertidal zone. In and of itself, if you ponder it deeply, this realization will tell you most everything you need to know about the primary cosmic function of the imaginal realm and our specific human contribution to this sphere of operations. But since these ideas may be very new to some of you not previously familiar with Gurdjieffian metaphysics, rest assured that I will circle back in chapter 3 and unpack them much more systematically.

I like this first map because it is *real*. Not only does it accord with a more contemporary understanding of the relationship between matter and energy, it also situates the whole unfolding *here* (admittedly a huge and vast "here") rather than in some mirage-like "spiritual" realm that floats "above" our visible solar system like a huge celestial theme park. It calls us to order, to a path of transformation that does not lead us away from materiality but straight into it and through it. Particularly when we enter those two lowest realms, *mi* and *re*, we are talking about our *actual* earth and our *actual* moon, and we are discussing planetary evolution along lines strikingly parallel to Teilhard de Chardin's. Nor will Gurdjieff let us off the hook here. For him, the major vehicle mediating that *mi-fa*

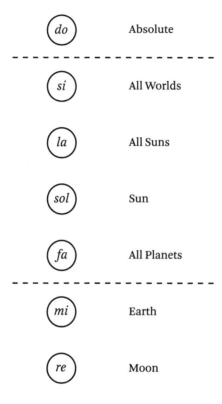

Gurdjieff's Ray of Creation

Adapted from P. D. Ouspensky,
In Search of the Miraculous: Fragments of an Unknown Teaching
(London: Harcourt, Inc., 1949), 82.

shock is the *biosphere*—yes, organic life on earth!—and its ultimate recipient is the *moon*, not our eternal souls. And yes, our conscious attention and willing participation will certainly make a huge difference in how our contribution is mediated and in which realm it is received. But willingly or unwillingly the tribute is exacted, and it is paid in the coin of *this* realm, in flesh and blood. Our inner work exists within the Megalocosmos and for the sake of the Megalocosmos, not the other way around; it is important never to forget this.

The Worlds

If the Ray of Creation is exterior and cosmic in its orientation, Gurdjieff's second map, his diagram of the worlds, is more interior. In Teilhardian terms, it describes the "within of things." You might think of it impressionistically as a "ray of being" running roughly parallel to the Ray of Creation while offering its own distinctive counterpoint. But again, bear in mind that these worlds (or "levels of consciousness," as we might be inclined to relabel them in the terminology of our own times) are not just interior or subjective experiences, but actual *spheres of causality*. In Gurdjieffian cosmology, the yang of it never quite drops out of sight.

As I mentioned earlier, from an external perspective the Gurdjieffian system seems to follow the classic sophia perennis model in that the worlds become progressively denser as one proceeds along the ray. A distinctive feature of this system, however, is that for Gurdjieff densification is not simply a matter of increasing "materiality" per se; it is rather that each realm comes under progressively more cosmic laws, i.e., constructal givens, that restrict its freedom and determine its outcomes. The higher "up" the ray, the fewer the cosmic laws. Our own world, near the bottom of the chain, operates under

	SCALE	LATIN NAME	COSMOLOGICAL LOCUS
2nd shock	do	_Do_minus	Holy Absolute; pre-big bang, "eternal cosmic inflation"
	⅔ ⅘		
	si	_Si_derum (All Stars)	The sum potential of all galaxies, all big bangs, all universes, now and forever
	la	_La_ctera (Milky Way)	Our galactic system
	sol	_Sol_ (Sun)	The center, or "Holy Absolute" of our own solar system
	fa	_Fa_tum (Fate)	The planets of our solar system
1st shock	⅔ ⅘		
	mi	_Mi_xtus Orbis (Mixed Realm)	Our planet Earth
	re	_Re_gina Coelis (Queen of Heaven)	The moon (youngest and most unstable element of the Ray)
	do$_2$	_Do_minus$_2$	The black hole at the end of the octave, occasioned by the implosion of our sun, which ends the development along this Ray, collapsing all back beneath the event horizon

The Ray of Creation:
A Contemporary Cosmological Interpretation

forty-eight laws (hence Gurdjieff's reference to it as "World 48"), which makes it a significantly dense and mechanical place. The imaginal, in its traditional positioning just "above" ours, is subject to twenty-four laws and hence is significantly more fluid and powerful. From there, the ray takes us back by successive halves to three, the primordial Trinity, and then to World 1, the undivided Holy Absolute. At each upward plateau there are fewer laws, but they are more binding.

I want to sketch these worlds for you as I have come to understand them. Rather than merely summarizing the attributes ascribed to them in the standard Gurdjieff/Ouspensky version[6] I will expand and occasionally completely redraw them. Some of these associations may be new to you (a few of them surprised me as well!). And while this "scenic route" may take us a little out of the way, I hope you will find the time well spent—if for no other reason than to reawaken a sense of wonder at "the scale of the thing," the utter vastness of the playing field upon which this cosmic drama unfolds. On a more practical level, these small thumbnails will serve as the functional basis for many otherwise "out of nowhere" connections I will be making from time to time in this book. You may find yourself referring back to them frequently, as I myself have already begun to do.

◯ World 1

World 1 is the Holy Absolute. The Godhead. The "inaccessible light," the holy impenetrable, ineffable, unknowable monad before "God took perceptivity and divisibility," as Jacob Boehme describes it.[7]

Of course, this is one of those giant forks in the road where the mystical traditions of the Christian East and Christian West split theologically. For the Western theological mind—with a few notable exceptions—there is no "Godhead behind God." The Trinity is the full, total, irreducible expression of the whole of divinity. The mystics of both branches, of course, have always smiled serenely at this. They know better.

This world corresponds with *do* on the Ray of Creation, or *dominus*—the Holy Absolute.

World 3

World 3 is the primordial ternary, whereby the Godhead—ever indivisible and unmanifest—brings himself into "perceptivity and divisibility," i.e., a "manipulable" inner configuration that will support "the impressure of nothing into something" (again, Boehme's words),[8] thus launching the long march toward outward manifestation. For both Boehme and Gurdjieff, this fundamental reconfiguration of the inner monadic ground inexorably requires three-ness, and what will emerge many worlds later as the theological doctrine of Trinity is in fact merely a distant echo of this more primordial upwelling of the Law of Three, rightly named by Gurdjieff as the "Law of World Creation." Indeed, following a brilliant lead handed to us by Boehme, we can say that it is only in this realm that one can properly begin to invoke the term "consciousness" (*con-scientia*, meaning "with-knowing"), because until there is a "with," there can be no "with-knowing" but only the bare, inscrutable will of the monad (which Boehme calls *scientia*). Consciousness is not the fundamental ground of all being. It is rather the first manifestation—which occurs in World 3—of perceptivity and divisibility. The two are joined at the hip.

This world corresponds with *si* on the Ray of Creation, or *siderum*—all the stars, all the galaxies, all possibilities, infinite possibilities.

World 6

This world launches the inaugural leap into outward manifestation, that first declension in Valentin Tomberg's spectrum of energy, where consciousness "condenses" into "psychic force" and begins to move as an actual energy stream, creating, animating, and shaping the created order. On traditional metaphysical maps it corresponds to what is known in the East as the "causal" and in the West as the "logoic."[9] By whatever name, it is primordial substantiality, the highest and most powerful expression of the pure creative *eros* that brings all things into being. It is the world that quivers into life when Teilhard writes, "The physical structure of the universe is love," or when he remarks, equally astoundingly, "Love is nothing more than the impressure, left in the heart of the creature, of the physical convergence of the universe."[10] Eros as logoic force, pure generativity, the blue of the flame in the heart of the monad. For J. G. Bennett, this is the demiurgic world from which the entire created order emerges. In the Gospel of John, this is "the Word." For that other John, my crazy, wild-hearted Greek, it is the *Zoi*, the pure life force, tugging against his entrails like a force 8 wind. The big bang is here; this is where our universe story begins. And while opinions may vary on this point, my own take is that it is the highest realm that can be directly touched and borne while still in human form. It is beyond personal; it is itself the great intertidal zone between the unmanifest and the primordial manifest. I would call it the true logoic realm: pure spirit, pure causality, pure eros moving untempered by any sort of human mediation like the wild, roving spirit font it can only be.

This world corresponds with *la* on the Ray of Creation, or *lactera*—the Milky Way, our galaxy; the place where it is all unfolding for us.

☀ *World 12*

World 12 is the Christic. I know this ascription may surprise some of you who are used to seeing "Christ Consciousness" positioned higher, as one of the nondual realms at the very top of the Great Chain of Being. I do not believe this is so. Even World 6, to my way of thinking, is already situated solidly within the causal or logoic bandwidth (*not* in the true nondual, which from a cosmological perspective denotes the unmanifest realms).

We have just seen above that World 6 bridges the gap between the manifest and unmanifest, and as its processionary offspring, World 12 would necessarily be subsumed within its overarching causality. Moreover, I concur with the ever-cage-rattling Bernadette Roberts in her insistence that "logos" and "Christ" are not the same, but rather, Christic is the "middle ground" (or mandorla, to give it its plane geometry name) that emerges in the overlapping zone between the human Jesus and the fiery divine logos[11]—between Worlds 24 and 6, if you want to put it that way. And that is a very good way to picture World 12. It is the world of fully incarnate and embodied love, the fullest of what bodhisattva consciousness can look like in form. It is the endpoint of the personal realms. And it is the world, I believe, in which we must locate what Teilhard envisions as the Omega Point, where all things are summed up in Christ—because this is the last world in which such a summation has any relevance. Beyond, all is summed up in logos. It is the *consummatum est* of a particularly rich and luminous outspeaking of the word *love*, emerging from the fires of eros to its transfigured fullness as agape. I will fill in some of these pieces in chapter 7.[12]

This world corresponds to *sol* on the Ray of Creation, or

the sun—the center of our solar system. From here emerges warmth, light, and cosmic ordering.

 ## *World 24*

World 24 is the "Kingdom of Heaven" as Jesus put it and supremely the home range of the imaginal. It is the world of *presence,* where the outer forms of physical materiality are illuminated from within by the light that pours from World 12 and above, and where human consciousness—awake, three-centered, and having passed that first conscious shock point (which it supremely tends and mediates)—fully inhabits this physical world, takes instructions reliably from the higher realms, and participates fully in the required cosmic exchange. This is the world of conscious man or woman—"man number four" in Gurdjieffian terminology—who lives awake and willing right there at the junction point where the "the two seas meet," infusing the staleness of the lower worlds with the vivifying energy of his or her authentic presence.

This world corresponds to *fa* on the Ray of Creation, or *fatum*—our immediate solar system.

 ## *World 48*

This is the "world" as we know it and transmit it through the best of human culture. It is the world of philosophy, ethics, and religion; the world of intellectual striving and cleverness and of industry, curiosity, science, technology, and the arts—in other words, the first fruits of civilization as best we know them. It is the world of high rationality. The world of high egoic functioning and self-reflective consciousness. The world that Teilhard mostly had in mind when he described the "noosphere." But for all its giftedness, it still falls just below that first conscious shock line; hence, it is still, in Gurdjieffian terms, preconscious and "asleep." It is Prospero's castle, entrancing and seductive, but ultimately a mirage.

This world corresponds to *mi* on the Ray of Creation, or the *mixtus orbis*. At its best, it symbolizes the fullest flourishing of the biosphere, the "Eden" of the Ray of Creation.

World 96

The thickening deepens. World 96 is the "formatory" world, as Gurdjieff calls it, where everything operates on autopilot, in clichés and thought-bites: stale, conditioned, habitual. There's not even any real thinking that goes on here, as there is in World 48; it's all recycled opinions and stereotypes. In Gurdjieffian terms, this is the world of personality, the world of "not-I"; of all that is artificially acquired and that obscures our real essence. It is monochrome, repetitive, and boring—uncreative, stony, and inanimate; the lowest world in which human consciousness can even barely hold its shape.

This world corresponds to *re* on the Ray of Creation, or *regina coeli*—the moon; pure geosphere, not yet able to support organic life; the youngest and most unstable element in the chain.

World 192

World 192 represents the hell realms. It is the world of the deeply disordered, anguished, and psychotic, the spawning ground of evil and the demonic, where consciousness has lost all spaciousness and congeals toward an unbearable density. The "bardo realms"—craving, wrath, pride, envy, and desire; obsession fixated to a deadly bullseye-turned-wormhole. Here self-reflective consciousness turns on itself like a rabid dog

biting its master. This is the final outpost before consciousness collapses into outer darkness—or simply goes comatose.
Cosmically, it is the collective pain body of humanity and of
the planet itself.

This world does not correspond to any point on the Ray of
Creation, but I envision it as the endpoint—the bottom *do*—
at which the entire octave has run its course and simply im-
plodes.

Below World 192, one can no longer properly speak of "consciousness." The Gurdjieffian maps continue on farther—to
an endpoint at 12,288—but by then we are well into the domain of inorganic chemistry. Some rudimentary sentiency
continues to exist into realms 384 and below, but these are
at the level of biological cellular function and not yet at the
threshold of anything measured along this second map, which
as we are working with it here could be described as comprising the "ray of consciousness."

The Imaginal World

From the foregoing descriptions, you have probably surmised
that I see the imaginal realm as quintessentially connected to
World 24. And that is indeed a fair surmise, provided you do
not fall into the trap of seeing it as a *separate* world, a world
even remotely comprehensible apart from the larger relational field it nests within. As we have spoken about before,
the essence of imaginal agency is that it is always interpenetrating and interanimating; it is *always* about connectivity.

And yes, the "central channel" of imaginal activity may indeed run through World 24. But if it does so, I would see this
operating in accordance with Gurdjieff's fundamental understanding of the Law of Three—"The higher blends with the

lower in order to activate the middle"—in which case, World 24 is simply "the middle." The entire range of the imaginal field of operations really spans the gamut between World 12, or the Christic, and World 48, our own distracted and not-yet-truly conscious earth plane. Through the lens of Christian mysticism I have come to envision it as a vast tempering ground in which the overpowering and essentially impersonal force of eros flowing from World 6 can be absorbed and safely transmitted to the lower realms, where it will undergo its ultimate transfiguration into agape through its investiture in finitude.

This is also, therefore, supremely the bandwidth of the *personal*—where, in the astonishing words of Ladislaus Boros, "The humanity of Christ has, as it were, absorbed, and thus neutralized the dangers of man's meeting with God."[13] Writ large, this triad of worlds is the mystical body of Christ, and the imaginal flows through it as its lifeblood.

While exchange between the realms occurs at every point along the Ray of Creation, there are certain features of this imaginal zone of operations that make it a particularly intense locus of activity. Let me simply summarize the three significant dovetails, collated in the composite schematic on the next page that provide such strong clues as to the specific nature of the exchange that goes on here.

First, running right across this extended bandwidth, separating Worlds 24 and 48, is that *first conscious shock*. This means that a new infusion of energy—or a different *kind* of energy—must be brought here in order to bridge the gap.

Second, straddling this same gap we find the junction point between what Tomberg calls "psychic force" ("radial energy" for Teilhard) and the more familiar world of "physical energy" ("tangential energy" for Teilhard). We move beyond the familiar realm of physical energy described under the Newtonian laws of thermodynamics into some new and subtler

	WORLD	SCALE	COSMOLOGICAL REALM	SPIRITUAL REALM
	1	*do*	Absolute	Holy Absolute
	3	*si*	All Worlds	Primordial Ternary
	6	*la*	All Suns	Logoic
	12	*sol*	Sun	Christic
	24	*fa*	All Planets	Kingdom of Heaven / Imaginal
	48	*mi*	Earth	Visible World
	96	*re*	Moon	Formatory World
	192	*do$_2$*	Sublunar	Hell Realms

Composite Map of the Worlds

bandwidth (classically associated with "prayer," "will," "love," and "attention"), which is also implicitly, according to Teilhard, counterentropic: it concentrates force rather than dissipating it.

Third, we are straddling the gap between preconscious and conscious in the Gurdjieffian sense: between man functioning merely as a highly sophisticated machine and man in the true sense of the term—balanced in all three centers, *present*, and manifesting at least the beginnings of conscience and real will.

Let's see how all this plays out when we throw ourselves into the mix.

Three

THE GREAT
EXCHANGE

Blessed is the Lion whom the man devours,
for that lion will become man. But cursed is the man whom
the lion devours, for that lion will become man.

—GOSPEL OF THOMAS, LOGION 7

IN THIS TINY, cryptic saying from the Wisdom teachings of Jesus we actually find the kernel of the entire complex Gurdjieffian notion of the Trogoautoegocrat laid out in less than thirty words. Certainly the moral kernel of it. Food, transformation, upward and downward exchange between the realms—it's all here, together with the stunningly unequivocal answer to the question, "What happens when we throw ourselves into the mix?" The answer is that we wind up in the eye of the needle.

In the first of these parallel, trompe l'oeil transformations, the man devours the lion, which means that he has digested, i.e., integrated, the fire and strength of his animal nature into the higher order of his conscious humanity; and the lion, thus transformed, steps forward as a servant and a vehicle. This is upward transformation. In the second, when the lion devours the man, the man simply loses himself in his lower order bestiality; his human consciousness and cleverness become servants for his primordial rage, and what emerges is chaos and destruction. This is *devolution*, the downward transformation. And as the saying ironically acknowledges, "that lion has now become man." It gets up in the morning, puts on its clothes, makes breakfast, makes policy, determines the fate of the world—and fills the atmosphere around him with the psychic toxins of his rage, fear, and alienation. This is "the terror of the situation," according to Gurdjieff. And we do not have to look far from our immediate world situation to see it playing out.

"The role of a conscious human being is to provide the phenomenal earth world with energies which otherwise would not be effectively transmitted to the creations and units which make up our world," writes William Segal, one of the most brilliant first-generation students of the Gurdjieff Work.[1] That is the bare, perhaps unglamorous bottom line. Whatever we like to *think* we're up to in our philosophical or spiritual fantasies—saving the world, saving our souls, attaining full enlightenment—in terms of cosmic exchange, we are *transformers*, of molecules and of meaning in equal measure. It is the cosmic function apportioned to us in the great Trogoautoegocrat. If we do it a certain way, something happens to us and to the planet; if we do it another way, something else happens.

All the world's spiritual traditions have tried to orient us rightly here through a fundamental baseline morality: "Do unto others as you would have them do unto you." Even in the absence of any further instructions, a simple adherence to the great moral precepts emerging from the first axial age will keep humans basically in right alignment to perform their required part in the great exchange. The transmission chain will flow smoothly. The lion will proceed toward man. But the shadow side of these ancient moral teachings is that they tend to rely on an individualized, fear-and-punishment-driven vision of an afterlife to motivate compliance. In the pervasively secular and skeptical culture of our times, where the fires of hell hold about as much clout as Santa or the tooth fairy, the human moral compass has increasingly defaulted to unabashed self-interest. "Go for the gusto!" "Get all you can get!" "You're *worth* it!" We all know the slogans; they are the mantras of our brave new world. And that is not merely a personal moral failure, claims Gurdjieff; it is an ecological catastrophe, for it amounts to a systemic breakdown, as across a broad sector of an entire pivotal species, "the lion devours the man," and the flow of those essential energies between the realms is destabilized.

Even at the turn of the last century Gurdjieff was already deeply concerned about what he saw to be a significant drop in the level of being required of our human species and hence of our ability to play our required part in the cosmic homeostasis. There's little question that the past hundred years of our planetary unfolding have more than borne out his concerns. When we collectively *devolve*, simply using our ambition and cleverness to live as successful lions, in that same downward spiral we fall below the critical threshold needed to maintain our place as "*conscious* human beings," the fundamental prerequisite for our full participation in the great exchange. When that function goes unperformed (or gets performed in a distorted or toxic way), it is not merely "our immortal souls" that suffer; the entire cosmic equilibrium is thrown out of whack.

I think we all sense in our bones that there is a closer and more organic connection than we would comfortably like to admit to between the kinds of energies we humans pump into the atmosphere as the fruit of our moral actions and the tangible effects of this "imaginal pollution" on the biosphere. We sense this, but we do not know why, for the traditional metaphysical maps are still based on outmoded science, and the modern scientific maps (with the notable exception of the one proposed by Teilhard de Chardin, who was at least bold enough to make a first stab at a new paradigm) do not yet integrate—or in most cases even *acknowledge*—the moral dimension implicit in all this. What does the handoff between radial and tangential energy actually look like? In what sense is human virtue an actual "food" supporting organic life on earth? And where and *how* in our own work of conscious transformation does the exchange between the realms actually get played out?

These are among the crucial missing pieces embedded in those overlapping diagrams of the worlds we started to consider in the previous chapter. In this chapter I will continue to explore this perhaps strange new way of fitting the pieces together in the hopes that it might open up a fresh angle of approach to some of the tragic impasses (intellectual, spiritual, ecological) of our own times. As we move beyond the traditional moral arguments into a closer look at the actual mechanics of the exchange that goes on here at this all-important *mi-fa* junction point, I think we will see with deepening resolve—and perhaps with deepening "remorse of conscience," as Gurdjieff would put it—why our human orientation toward the good is not a personal virtue but a collective cosmic responsibility.

A Brief Note on "Up" and "Down"

Before heading further into the material of this chapter, I need to clarify a potential source of confusion here so that it does not trip us up. In another of those unavoidable trompe l'oeils, there are actually *two* kinds of "up" and "down" we'll be looking at, and it's important to keep them sorted out. The first is the evolution/devolution polarity we've just been considering here; in this case "up" means toward a higher state of being (lion becomes man) and "down" means to a lower one (man becomes lion). But there is a second meaning of "up" and "down" at play here, which turns out to factor even more significantly in our exploration of reciprocal feeding—namely, the legitimate and necessary "uploading" and "downloading" of energies between the realms. In this second case *each* direction of movement is equally essential to the overall equilibrium. As we proceed through the material, I will try to be clear about the sense in which I am using these directional markers; it is really in the interplay between them that the fuller picture begins to emerge.

Imaginal Mechanics

So how does the exchange between the realms actually work? The hidden driveshaft lies in that small piece of information I slipped in toward the end of the previous chapter: in Gurdjieffian cosmological theory, density is created not so much by physical materiality per se as by the number of laws to which that realm is bound. Our earth plane, World 48, operates under forty-eight causal laws. The imaginal realm, operating fundamentally as World 24, is half as dense and so twice as free, twice as fluid.

These "laws" are of course not rules in a juridical sense; they are more like algorithms governing the conventions by which each realm is constructed. In our earth realm, they include such stipulations as linear time, diachronic (sequential) causality, corporeal density, a nucleated sense of selfhood, "attraction/aversion" as the core behavioral motivator, a pervasive underlying sense of scarcity and either/or-ness (it's built right into the mental hardwiring through which we perceive the world), and a compulsory fealty to the laws of gravity and entropy. Collectively these parameters call into being a world that is solid in its outward appearance but rather sluggish and plodding in its actual modus operandi. We get there, but it takes us awhile.

In the imaginal realm, the governing principles are synchronous causality, radial time, nonduality, fluid and permeable boundaries, nonlocalized action, a holographic sense of selfhood (the whole in the part and the part in the whole), conscience as the core behavioral motivator, and a capacity to move against the flow of entropy and actually generate energy rather than merely dissipate it.

Because of the markedly different densities of these two adjoining realms, items sharing the same name prove to have significantly different configurations. In this earth realm my *body* is understood to be the flesh-and-blood structure that defines the functional boundaries of "me" and is the seat of my individual personhood. The *energy* that basically runs the place is tangential or physical, the energy described by physics under the laws of thermodynamics. The essential *qualities* of my humanness and everybody else's humanness are seen basically as simply "virtues" or "vices," essential descriptors of our character, but in the end adjectives, nothing more.

It is not so in the imaginal realm.

In this lighter, more fluid realm, my *body,* as we have seen already, is not the outer shell but a more subtle inner body— identified variously in the esoteric traditions as the "subtle body," "inner body," "second body," or "kesdjan body"—and registering in World 48 as simply that quality of inner aliveness I have spoken of already, the live snake slithering in the grass. The operative *energy* here is primarily radial—finer, quicker, diffusive, and more intense and purposive. And in this more fluid world, those aforementioned virtues and vices become *subtle cosmic substances*—not merely thought forms but actual chemical elements needed for the building up (or, alas, tearing down) of our World 48 and the worlds below it on the chain.

So the work really consists in the conversion of energy between these two density gradients. And that work goes on principally through the mediating vehicle of our uniquely human form of consciousness.

World 48	World 24
linear time	radial / spatial time
sequential causality	synchronous causality
either-or dualism	nonduality
corporeal density	fluid and permeable boundaries
nucleated selfhood	holographic selfhood
attraction/aversion	conscience
entropic	counterentropic
tangential energy	radial, generative energy
flesh-and-blood body	subtle inner body
virtue as descriptor	virtue as operative energy

Teilhard de Chardin grasped this point vividly. Though completely unfamiliar (so far as we know) with the teachings of Western esotericism, he was in the 1920s already clearly perceiving from a scientific perspective that what we call the "theological virtues" are actually *streams of radial energy* changing outcomes in the physical world. In his *The Divine Milieu* he insists that faith is "operative," meaning for him that it actually acts in this world, changing not only the outcome but *the subtle physical composition of materiality*. As he sees it, "Under the influence of faith, the universe is capable, without outwardly changing its characteristics, of becoming more supple, more fully animate, of becoming sur-animated."[2] No doubt unbeknownst to Teilhard, this is a remarkably precise definition of imaginal causality as it would be classically understood in the Inner traditions of the West (essentially as we saw it summarized by Walter Wink in chapter 1). And Teilhard takes this definition even a step further with his insight that the agent of change here is not merely an awakened human heart acting upon the world, but *faith itself acting upon the world* through a direct energetic impact upon the molecular elements of which the world is comprised.

I was on to this same intuition fifteen years ago, although at the time I did not have either the imaginal or Teilhardian language under my belt. What I *did* sense keenly, however, when I first tackled the subject in *The Wisdom Way of Knowing*, is that the cosmic task we humans were called upon to perform was uniquely alchemical in nature and that it had to do with releasing the vivifying and generative properties that belong properly to the higher realms into the bloodstream of our own "sensible" realm. What I then referred to as "the names of God coiled within the physical form of things" I might now reimagine as World 24 coiled within World 48; in either case, the marching orders remain the same.

In chapter 5 of that book, I ease into describing the energetic nature of this exchange by means of the image of a candle, whose outward form is of course tallow and wick, but whose inner essence is flame—revealed, however, only when the match is struck and the candle starts to burn. I then continue:

> We are talking about transformation, of course, a kind of sacred alchemy. And it is precisely this alchemy that defines our essential human task. The secret of our identity does not lie in the outer form or in how successfully

we manipulate the forms of the sensible world. Rather, it lies in how we are able to set them (and ourselves) aflame to reveal the inner quality of their aliveness. The names of God lie coiled within the physical forms of things; our particular and uniquely human task is to spring the trap and set them free. They cannot manifest apart from the sensible realm (that's what the sensible realm is here for), but neither will they manifest automatically within it unless there is a further act of conscious transformation. That is our job.[3]

In this early run-up on the subject, I already sensed the lineaments of an upward and downward transmission—downward in this sense meaning not devolution (lion eats man), but rather the legitimate flow of elements generated in the higher realms into the lower ones as animating and generative energies. This is what William Segal was referring to in the passage earlier cited when he spoke of "energies which otherwise would not be effectively transmitted to the creations and units which make up our world." But this downward transmission paradoxically entails an upward transmission as well, for to make its way unimpeded across the crucial *mi-fa* hesitation point requires the infusion of a different *kind* of energy, of a subtly different and finer quality, flowing in a different direction. That is the enormous cosmic gift potentially ours to give as we become increasingly willing to set fire to the tallow-and-wick of our outer lives in order to release the heat and fragrance coiled within. If you translate *heat* as "radial energy," and *fragrance* as "conscious attention," you will have a strong intimation of what William Segal is talking about when he writes several paragraphs later: "Without the upward transmission of energies through the intermediary of conscious attention, the universe would give in to entropy."

The Eucharist as Imaginal Exchange

We do not need to look far afield to find a powerful working image of what I mean by "the conversion of energy between two density gradients." It's all right there in the central Mystery of the Christian faith, the Eucharist.

I am intentionally calling it a Mystery here—not simply a "ritual" or even a "sacrament"—because I believe that Christianity is fundamentally all about the exchange between the realms, and the Eucharist is one of the central channels through which this exchange flows. In it all the elements we have been talking about so far—reciprocal feeding, transformation, upward and downward transmission—are powerfully concentrated, so that when we gaze deeply into its mirror, we are also gazing deeply into a hologram of the entire cosmic Trogoautoegocrat. The two can thus be used fruitfully to unpack and clarify each other.

Let's see what the Eucharist looks like when viewed through the lens of imaginal exchange. We begin with bread and wine, two physical "bodies" from our earth plane, World 48. Through the power of our conscious intentionality, meeting with the conscious intentionality of Christ, they are transformed into "body" and "blood" as they actually manifest in World 24, i.e., as more subtly embodied cosmic substances that flow into us as we "consume" him, nourishing our own subtle inner body, our true vehicle for continuous communication between the realms.

Meanwhile, at the same time that we are consuming him, he is also consuming us—and we find ourselves literally "lions devoured by the Man," upwardly transposed and digested into his infinitely greater wholeness in order to take our place briefly in World 12, the mystical body of Christ. Thus nurtured and transformed (that's the theory of it, anyway), we return to our own World 48 as viaducts of those transformed Christic fruits—peace, gentleness, love, patience, joy, love, kindness, forbearance, self-control[4]—which then flow from us out into the physical world to make it "more supple, more fully animate." And this state of heightened, flowing, communicative aliveness would in turn be a good way of describing the "Kingdom of Heaven": World 24 causality realized within the finite boundaries of World 48. As Jesus in the Gospel of Thomas picturesquely envisions this holographic unity:

> He who drinks what flows from my mouth
> Will come to be like me
> And I will come to be like him
> So that all may be one.[5]

The Eucharist thus reveals itself to be a single, unbroken tri-realmic loop whose cosmic purpose is to maintain a unified field of Christic love across the entire spectrum of the personal realms.

Tools for the Journey

This new way of framing the picture significantly shifts our understanding of spiritual practice. While traditional religious teaching has typically pictured our spiritual task as freeing ourselves from the lower realms in order to secure our placement in a higher one, through the lens of imaginal exchange this turns out to be at best a partial truth. It is indeed fair to say that if I wish to be a conscious participant in the greater cosmic exchange while still physically living in World 48, I must realize my citizenship in World 24, for that is where authentic human consciousness actually begins. But this realization is not in order to "leave" this world, but rather to *fully occupy it*;

to stand awake and present in that *mi-fa* gap and there make my offering to the greater cosmic ecology.

According to Gurdjieff, the two vehicles par excellence for actualizing this inner transformation are *conscious labor* and *intentional suffering*. I have spoken about them in many other places in my writing, but for those of you who are unfamiliar with this duo, at least a brief introduction is in order here. Conscious labor is basically any intentional effort that moves against the grain of entropy, i.e., against that pervasive tendency of human consciousness to slip into autopilot. It means summoning the power of conscious attention (in our era perhaps more widely known as "mindfulness") to swim upstream against that pervasive lunar undertow drawing us toward stale, repetitive, mechanical patterns, the siren call of World 96. In the words of the Khwajagan, the Central Asian Masters of Wisdom, whose teachings were near and dear to Gurdjieff's heart, "Be present with every breath; do not let your attention wander for the space of a single breath."[6] Or in a passage from Maurice Nicoll, near and dear to Rafe's heart, the work amounts to "a continual inner effort, a continual altering of the mind, of the habitual ways of thought, of the habitual ways of taking everything, of habitual reactions."[7] Whether the effort is as modest as simply noticing a negative emotion rather than blindly reacting or as heroic as struggling with an addiction, it is not the scale of the undertaking but the honesty of the struggle that reverses the direction of flow.

If conscious labor increases our capacity to stay present, intentional suffering radically increases the heartfulness of that presence. Operating in a slightly different quadrant of the human psyche but with a parallel strategy of reversing the direction of flow, intentional suffering goes head-to-head with that well-habituated pattern (again, one of the constructal givens of World 48 and below) to move toward pleasure and away from pain. It invites us to step up to the plate and willingly carry a piece of that universal suffering, which seems to be our common lot as sentient beings in a very dense and dark corner of the universe. The size of the piece does not matter. It can be as small (though not easy!) as "bearing another human being's unpleasant manifestations," as Gurdjieff was fond of reminding people. It can be as vast as "greater love has no man than to lay down his life for his neighbor."

What does matter, however, is that the suffering must be *intentional*, i.e., conscious, clear, and impartial. He is not talking about the useless and completely avoidable suffering caused by the frustration of our neurotic programs and illusions, what one of my Buddhist friends picturesquely describes as "squeezing the cactus." Gurdjieff himself called it "stupid suffering." This is simply the laws of Worlds 96 and 192 playing out, and it is of no redemptive value whatsoever to the wider cosmic ecology. To qualify as upwardly transformative work, the offering must be *pure* (free of personal gain or self-interest); it must be *spacious* (nonurgent and unattached to outcome); and it must be *generous* (offered on behalf of the larger whole). Then it does its work very well.

To my way of looking at it, intentional suffering is a very high practice. I believe it does not fundamentally belong to World 24 but emanates from a yet higher world, from World 12, where it bears the energy of the Christic or bodhisattva consciousness, the fully awakened heart that knows we are all in this together and that there is in fact no "other." When undertaken rightly, it is always implicitly paschal. At the upper end its vibrational field begins to resonate with the energy of World 6, where universal suffering metamorphizes into a causal principle—"pain is the ground of motion," as Jacob Boehme bluntly put it[8]—and the sufferings of the created order meet their uncreated prototype in the suffering of God.

And do not think that this is just sentimental suffering over the misery we humans inflict on ourselves and one another through the misuse of our freedom. It is that, but it is far more than that; it is in the end a kind of primordial cosmic constant, the necessary cost of the "impressure of nothing into something," which is borne directly in the marrow of the divine heart as World 1 allows itself to be drawn and quartered so that all other worlds may come into being. Gurdjieff would speak of this allusively from time to time, most openly in his fourth Obligolnian Striving,[9] where he averred that our real human task was "to pay as quickly as possible for one's arising and individuality in order afterward to be free to lighten as much as possible the sorrow of our Common Father." The words are simple, but when you catch the deep love and cosmic sadness flowing through them, there is no response other than tears. This is the Omega Point of the path of intentional suffering; from here we can go no further.

Conscious labor and intentional suffering are not so much separate practices as twin pillars of what amounts to essentially a single spiritual obligation (Gurdjieff called it our "being-Partkdolg-duty"). They dovetail well with the classic spiritual practices of mindfulness and surrender (conscious labor equates to mindfulness, and intentional suffering, seen through the paschal lens, is quintessentially surrender). Together they position us well to live here in World 48 under the laws of World 24—or in other words, under the sway of imaginal causality. And this would in fact be a very good way to make sense of Jesus's admonition to be "in this world but not of it." As we work with these tools, we gradually develop the willingness and capacity to sacrifice our self-actualization under the laws of "the lower forty-eight" in order that the raw materials of our surrendered will and personal drama can instead be transformed into something of imperishably finer substantiality. That is the authentic possibility set before us and at the same time our most difficult challenge.

The Options

In which realm will I choose to play out my hand? Worlds 48 and 96 are essentially nonchoices, merely the path of least resistance. This is our default human "home range," and all the currents of our collective cultural heritage set toward keeping it in place. Here we will certainly find more than enough to keep us occupied and distracted for the relatively short span of our human lives and to weave the narrative of our personal "soul journey." But in the end, what will have been accomplished? From the perspective of the greater cosmic ecology a very different picture emerges. If I choose to play out my life under the laws of this earth plane, according to Gurdjieff (whether in World 48 or World 96; energetically it makes no appreciable difference), I may indeed work very hard to be a good and responsible citizen. I may move a lot of pieces around on the playing field of this life and reap my share of the rewards to be gained here: fame, respect, fortune, the illusion of security. But in terms of making any enduring contribution to the cosmic exchange, it's pretty much a wash. The good and the harm that I do basically cancel each other out, at least when weighed in the collective balance: which is the only way our contribution can be weighed, for at this level of human evolution true individuality does not yet exist. For the greater purposes of the Trogoautoegocrat, I am not yet even in the ball game, for down here in the lower realms, it's all just *do-re-mi, do-re-mi*. The threshold into conscious participation is crossed at *fa*, World 24. Below that threshold, my contribution is exacted unconsciously and involuntarily, again according to the laws of World 48: when I die, my earthly body, together with its still largely undeveloped imaginal or inner body (the true seat of my "soul," or permanent individuality) will simply dissolve back into its constituent elements and become part of the overall energy of the biosphere—as Gurdjieff pungently puts it, "food for the moon." Nothing is wasted.

For one hundred years now that teaching has made people squirm. For Christians in particular it feels like a direct affront to our cherished notion of an immortal soul—and of course, that's exactly what it is, for in Gurdjieff's take we do not arrive here with an already furnished soul; soul is rather the supreme fruit of our earthly sojourn, forged in the refiner's fire of our conscious labor and intentional suffering. I am not about to legislate in this venerable dispute—only to note that, from the point of view of hedging our bets as well as for doing the maximum potential cosmic good, it's a far safer prospect to assume that we don't yet have one and then work sincerely toward its attainment than to assume that we *do* and simply coast on our laurels (as we Christians have been doing for two thousand years now), leaving our planet further and further in the lurch.

Upward Mobility

If and when I make that other, more difficult choice, to play out my hand here as best I can under the laws of World 24, a whole different scenario is set in motion. As I am increasingly able to assume my place as a conscious participant in the great exchange, there are some salient differences in the way my contribution is offered and processed, which actually paint a much more hopeful picture, both for myself and for the cosmos in which I am embedded.

The most significant of these is that my required cosmic contribution is exacted not at the hour of my death but in *the ongoing alchemy of my life,* through the catalytic force of my conscious work. This may well be what the Sufi mystics are alluding to when they speak of "dying before you die." It definitely implies that "man eats lion" at a critical new threshold. Rather than simply integrating my shadow elements into my phenomenal selfhood (as this process tends to be understood here in the psychological climate of World 48), I instead offer *my entire phenomenal selfhood* as the "lion" to be consumed and integrated under the higher causality of World 24. The materials of my life from which in the lower worlds one constructs the metanarrative of self (my history, my passions, my drama, etc.) become instead the raw material to be transformed into far higher order cosmic substances: "food for the earth" rather than "food for the moon."

By "higher order cosmic substances" I am referring primarily to those aforementioned "fruits of the spirit"—love, joy, peace, forbearance, kindness, goodness, faithfulness, gentleness, and self-control. From the fountain of our surrendered being they flow out into our immediate earth environment, where they do indeed help it to become "more supple, more fully animate," more responsive—more *personal,* Teilhard would say—less toxic and indifferent, more a place where sentient beings can flourish and grow.

At the same time, however, two related processes are also going on. The first is that this conscious transformation simultaneously releases *radial energy,* which is counterentropic and furnishes the required infusion of a "new or qualitatively different kind of energy" to carry the upward and downward flow along the Ray of Creation through the critical *mi-fa* shock point. It is to this function that William Segal is referring, I believe, in his aforementioned statement: "Without the upward transmission of energies through the intermediary of conscious attention, the universe would give in to entropy."

As the alchemical byproduct of this first process, what gradually begins to form within me is none other than that "second" or "kesdjan" body, a different and subtler vehicle for my aliveness. Remember this is what "body" actually means in imaginal causality, and since its arising is under the laws of the higher-order causality, it already has currency in the higher realms and allows me to navigate there, beyond the conventions of time and physical death, which set the boundaries of our usual earth plane. It will serve increasingly as the seat of my real selfhood and my vehicle for my engagement with the wisdom and cosmic assistance that flows to us from these realms. It is what Gurdjieff really has in mind when he speaks of developing a soul.

Food for the moon, or food for the earth? One way or another, we will all wind up as food—but for which realm? As it was regularly pointed out in the Fourth Way group I participated in for nearly a decade, there is really only one choice awaiting us in this earth realm: whether we will serve out our time here as an "unconscious slave" or a "conscious servant." If we elect the former, it all runs mechanically to its end, and the harvest is reaped in the biosphere. If we elect the more difficult second route—the conscious labor and intentional suffering that activates our full imaginal citizenship, we will sooner or later take up our duties in what Gurdjieff called "the conscious circle of humanity," offering the fruit of our conscious labor for the collective nurturance and protection of our still all-too-tender-and-fragile planet—and, yes, to lighten the sorrow of our Common Father.

In my own journey, that was the divide I stepped over, certainly not fully knowing what I was doing, when I met Rafe. Up to that point the Work ideas had lived in me still mostly at the level of interesting theories. Not so for Rafe. By the time I met him, he had already been walking the path for more than forty years. Every day up in his hermit cabin, along with his Bible, he read Maurice Nicoll's *Psychological Commentaries on the Teachings of Ouspensky and Gurdjieff.* The passages on the inner body were always well thumbed and marked, and indeed the book was open to one of these pages on the day that he died. He aspired to the conscious circle; he took his cues from this imaginal and lived under its laws with a consistency that terrified most weaker souls. And he took seriously the instruction he discerned that I had been entrusted to him as his charge in the transmission chain. He never backed off it.

"Perhaps that's what we've been brought together for," he pondered one day on a drive home from a doctor's appointment, not long before his death. "To form a connection from here to eternity."

I thought he was just being romantic.

THE HELL REALMS

TRAGICALLY, A THIRD option is always with us: the lion eats the man, and things keep right on spiraling downward, through the deepening rigor mortis of World 96 into the toxic and pathological constriction of World 192, the hell realms. Yes, I know a bit about those places now, too—way more than I would ever have wanted to know, sanguine and sheltered soul that I am. Who would have thought that the real destination of my winter odyssey with the Greek would be straight into these realms? But as I watched the escalating pathology between us, I could begin to see only too well how evil grows full-blown from the innocent soil of human hurt and pain, and how we humans, compulsory transformers that we are, will transform that as well.

I was stubborn—way too stubborn—in my commitment to the ideal that through love man always winds up eating the lion. But that's only true if what's being generated is actually love. As the magnetic disturbance in the energy field between us continued to grow once John had arrived back in Stonington for the summer, it became inescapably clear that the lion was eating the man in both of us; we were both being taken down. And as those magnetic waves of disturbance finally leaped the boundaries of our personal relationship and began to fan out in widening waves of agitation within our own community, I realized tragically that the game had gone too far.

One does not have the right, even in the name of love, to add to the already swollen pain body of our common humanity.

And it must be said, alas, that a lot of the work of the conscious circle of humanity lies in the daily dialysis of this toxic pain that our crazy, unreconciled, untamed lion/human consciousness inflicts on the planet, oil thrown on the fire of the divine eros, which is already quite fiery enough. No, the pathway toward real love, not this crazy craving stuff, lies in the opposite direction—and I would like to think it is as true for our Common Father as it is for Johnny and me—when that fiery eros which is at once the driveshaft and the ultimate anguish of the entire Ray of Creation sinks down, deep in these finite realms, and submits to its own transfiguration into agape in the cradle of the surrendered human heart.

Four

IMAGINAL
CAUSALITY

I HAVE BEEN living under the sway of imaginal causality for
nearly twenty-five years now, more than a third of my life. It's
been a kind of dual citizenship, not always easy to manage.
I got catapulted there, willy-nilly, in those raw weeks following Rafe's death, when something in me decided not to close
things out and move on but to keep on walking with him into
the unknown, a baby bloodhound following a scent trail I
could just barely recognize. He had given me one clue: "You
must trust the invincibility of your heart." But my heart at that
point seemed far from invincible. Still full of gaping holes,
deep in grief, and virtually untrained in subtle perception, it
was prone to all sorts of distortions. I made my way mostly by
trial and error.

Since then, I've been gradually learning the lay of the land,
and of course it's the fruits of that bushwhacking I want to
share with you here in this book, in the hope that they will en-
courage still further bushwhacking on your own. If, as I suggested in the previous chapter, the way we can really show up
for cosmic service boils down to learning to live in World 48
under the laws of World 24, how do we actually learn to do
this? What makes imaginal causality so distinctively different from our familiar World 48 causality? What are its telltale

features, and how do we get up to speed in a whole new operating system working at half the constraint but double the intensity? These will be the questions under consideration in the next two chapters.

I want to begin by looking at the big picture—because that's what imaginal causality actually is, a *big picture*. The first and most important thing to keep in mind about it is that it is spatial, not linear. Linear causality is a governing convention only for World 48 and below; above this threshold that pervasive, metronomic sense of the flow of time simply drops out. And this premise is verifiable, incidentally, not only in the domain of metaphysics but as a foundational understanding of quantum physics as well; beyond the confines of a rather narrow bandwidth of space-time in which Newtonian physics holds true, time ceases to have any functional meaning and proves itself to be simply one of the conventions that allows this particular earth plane to function. It is easily superseded, and at the junction with the imaginal, it is decisively overturned.[1]

What takes its place? There are many ways of picturing this transition, but my favorite is still the one I came up with myself many years ago when I was just starting to wrap my mind around these things. I shared it first in my book *Mystical Hope*, but here's the replay: One Sunday many years ago when I was living on an island off the coast of Maine, I put my teenage daughter Lucy on a ferry to the mainland four miles away to meet her boyfriend Scott. Then, since the day was exceptionally clear and calm, I went up on a high bluff on my own island to watch the whole little drama play out. I saw each of the sequences unfolding in turn: the ferry approaching the dock, Scott's little yellow Toyota moving down the landing road, and, in my mind's eye at least, Lucy moving to the front of the ferry, all eager to disembark and meet up with Scott. For the two of them, these events were being lived in time. But from my vantage point they were all present already, all contained in a huge, stately "now."

That's basically the key to reading imaginal causality: you learn to shift your perspective from that of a passenger on the ferry to the broader view awaiting you on the high bluff.

Intuitive as always, Teilhard de Chardin comes very close to naming this same reality in his remarkable preface to *The Human Phenomenon*, tellingly titled "To See." He describes how we humans are typically trapped within our own horizontal field of perspective, looking at things "objectively," so we think, but always and only at eye level. "It is only normal, but confining, for us to have to carry with us wherever we go the center of the landscape we are passing through," he acknowledges. But *then*, he ponders:

> What would happen to us, walking, if the chances of our journey brought us to a naturally advantageous panoramic point (an intersection of roads or valleys) from which not only our eyes looked out, but from which things themselves radiate? Then, as the subjective point of view coincided with the objective distribution of things, perception would be established in its fullest. The landscape would become legible and illuminated from within. We would see.[2]

Teilhard seems to be picturing this "naturally advantageous panoramic point" only in terms of an exterior topos ("an intersection of roads or valleys"), something on the outer plane. But on the inner plane he has once again just hit the nail on the head. For in the interior topography of consciousness, imaginal causality is indeed the higher vantage point, energetically/causally, from which things themselves radiate. This is so because, as we have seen, the imaginal is causative (or at least *generative*) with respect to World 48; it contains the epicentric point from which all things radiate outward into this slower sphere of causality (or to follow the stream in the opposite direction, the point at which they converge). To see from this point of view is indeed no longer merely "subjective," for "the subjective point of view coincide[s] with the objective distribution of things." The inner is like the outer, as in the celebrated logion 22 in the Gospel of Thomas, and from this causal point one can indeed "replace a hand with a hand and a foot with a foot, making one image supersede another."[3] One does indeed *see*—imaginally, that is. A more concise and accurate description of imaginal causality can hardly be conceived.

Chiasm

Because of this fundamentally spatial aspect of imaginal causality, the bits and pieces inside the frame do not usually hook up in a linear fashion. More often they appear as simultaneous, overlapping resonances or patterns, caught by the heart rather than the mind, speaking in the language of resonance, or "correspondences" as the poet Baudelaire called them, announcing their logic by the strength of the connectivity they establish between them. Typically, this manifests from our earth-plane perspective as a series of meaningful coincidences or a striking synchronicity, and these features are indeed the primary hallmark of imaginal causality at play.

But while this impression is technically correct—coincidence and synchronicity do indeed feature prominently in imaginal causality—the overall picture we get from the description tends to be misleading, for to our usual way of hearing these words, they seem to depict random, extraordinary, or exceptional (even weird) events, and this part is manifestly *not* true. When the higher-vibrational laws of the imaginal realm bleed through into this earth plane, they can and do strike us as extraordinary, but they really are not; they are simply following the rigorous constructal logic of that higher realm, a different and more subtle way of making connections. There is always an underlying pattern.

So I would like to begin this exploration of imaginal causality with a closer look at this underlying pattern. And I would propose even more specifically that we begin by focusing on a particular kind of pattern—known as chiasm—which seems to factor mightily in the imaginal delivery systems and thus gives us a very good starting point for beginning to learn this new way of making connections. While it may be stretching things to say that imaginal causality is inherently chiastic, it does seem to have a strong proclivity in this direction, and a closer inspection of two of its most well-loved specimens gives us an excellent opportunity to see how the whole system works. If nothing else, it moves us swiftly beyond the impression that imaginal interaction with our own world is merely by means of extraneous "signs and wonders"; the whole field is very tightly interwoven.

Chiasm is a traditional literary form, but the design principle is equally applicable in music and the visual arts. It consists of paired events arranged symmetrically around a center core. The simplest form is B, A, B', with A representing the center and B the symmetrical wings. The next more complicated level is C, B, A, B', C', and the sequence continues on from there. You can see the basic pattern; it's essentially a stone thrown into a pond with concentric circles fanning out around it.

Chiasm is a whole different way of ordering causality, and a good way of illustrating it might be by means of a familiar gospel story: the tale of Zacchaeus the tax collector up in a tree (Luke 19:1–7). In this brief incident, Zacchaeus, who is quite a short man and can't see over the crowd, runs on ahead and climbs a sycamore tree to catch a glimpse of Jesus as he enters town. Jesus spots him there and immediately calls out, "Zacchaeus, hurry and come down, for I must stay at your house today." Linear causality allows us two options for why this happens: (1) Zacchaeus's climbing a tree causes Jesus to spot him there and invite him for a private audience or (2) Jesus's prior, prescient knowledge that it is appointed for him to spend time with Zacchaeus causes the man to climb the tree. You can play it either way, but in imaginal causality a third option presents itself; namely, that there is a clear, necessary, and *already imaginally existent reality* of their two hearts deeply joined; that is A, the center. Around that, the Bs happen synchronously and

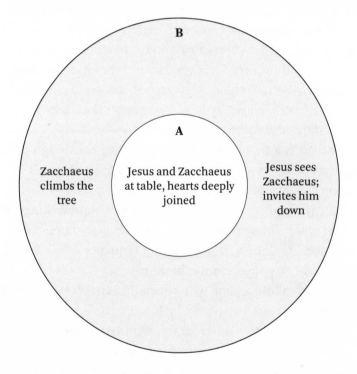

Jesus and Zacchaeus in Chiastic Form

effortlessly: Zacchaeus climbs the tree and Jesus spots him there and invites him down. Both men play their parts flawlessly, like subject and countersubject in a Bach fugue, woven together as a single harmonic whole around a unified, purposive core. That is what the world looks like under the lens of imaginal causality.

Perhaps my most comprehensive introduction to chiasm as a foundational principle of imaginal design came via a book that changed my life: *The Good Wine*, by my longtime monastic mentor at the New Camaldoli Hermitage in Big Sur, California, Bruno Barnhart.[4] First published in 1993, it is a complex, brilliant, imaginal reconstruction of the Gospel of John on the basis of chiasm. The book takes off from an earlier scholarly study of chiasm in the Gospel of John, *The Genius of John* by Peter Ellis—but it takes off like a rocket blasting into outer space! While Ellis's work still colors largely within the lines of established Old Testament historical/critical methodology, Bruno dives deep into the cave of his heart to come up with his own profoundly mystical commentary, a biblical Prospero's castle blown to cosmic proportions.

I want to hunker down with this text for a bit here, not only because time spent with the Gospel of John is never time misspent, but because it gives us a chance to look more closely at some of the distinctive features of imaginal causality as it plays out beneath the narrative surface of this world. On the linear level, the Gospel of John consists of twenty-one chapters leading us sequentially through the earthly ministry of Jesus, his crucifixion, resurrection, and post-resurrection appearances. Beneath the linear sequence, however, Bruno detects a complex, seven-ringed chiastic structure through which the gospel proves to be allusively telling a *second* story: of Jesus as the Lord and cornerstone of the New Creation. Those seven rings correspond to a highly configured re-creation of the original seven days of the Genesis story, and as those formerly sequential narrative segments fall into a whole new symmetrical configuration and begin speaking to each other from within this new configuration, they cumulatively resonate with the message that in Jesus the earth has been foundationally reborn and placed under a new headship.

Chiastic construction begins, of course, with finding the center, and Bruno unhesitatingly locates it in that short, mysterious vignette in John 6:16–21 where Jesus suddenly appears to his disciples walking upon the water:

> When evening came, his disciples went down to the lake, got into a boat, and started across the lake to Capernaum. It was now dark and Jesus had not yet come to them. The lake became rough because a strong wind was blowing. When they had rowed about three or four miles, they saw Jesus walking on the lake and coming near the boat, and they were terrified. But he said to them, "It is I; do not be afraid." Then they wanted to take him into the boat and the boat reached the land toward which they were going.

In his selection of this passage as chiastic center, he is following Peter Ellis, but for a very different reason: for Ellis the passage evokes the historical Exodus; for Bruno it resonates with the primordial watery chaos at that dawn of creation. This powerfully concentrated archetypal image thus furnishes the Rosetta stone for the entire New Creation mandala, and this is exactly what a chiastic center does and why it is in fact the center. It is almost always a brief, iconic wormhole into the imaginal epicenter that will in fact be driving the causality as things ring out into time.

With his center established and Rosetta stone in hand, it is not a difficult leap (at least for a mind like Bruno's) to establish the seven concentric rings and reallocate the narrative material accordingly. The full results of this process are packed into the diagram on page 74, but what is most interesting to me is the new groupings that emerge and the new conversations that flow from them. Day 4, for example, unfolds around the theme of "You are the light of the world" (since the fourth day of creation in the Genesis account features the establishment of the sun and the moon) and brings together Nicodemus (John 3:1–21), the man born blind (John 9:1–41), and Jesus's own Farewell Discourse (John 13–17) in a conversation about teaching, empowerment, and the true source of vision. Day 5, whose theme is "life" (this is the day in Genesis when the biosphere emerged in all its creaturely splendor), features a fascinating symmetrical grouping of the raising to life of the centurion's son (John 4:43–54), the raising of Lazarus (John 10–11), and Jesus's own passion (John 18–19). Particularly lovely to me is his Day 6, which manages to clump together the four feminine pericopes—the wedding at Cana (John 2:1–12), the woman at the well (John 4:4–42), the anointing at Bethany (John 12:1–11), and Mary Magdalene in the garden (John 20:1–18)—in a single, symphonic infusion of the feminine energy, celebrating, in Bruno's words, that "the feminine principle in the world is the inexhaustible source of creative realizations of the Father's glory."[5] Through this rapturous chiastic interenfolding, passages widely separated from each other in the linear narrative come into spontaneous, synchronous dialogue, reverberating like bells in a bell rack. The resulting music is simply, well, *elegant!*[6]

Resonance

In imaginal causality the meaning is generated in the richness of the interplay. One can speak, properly, about a "tapestry of

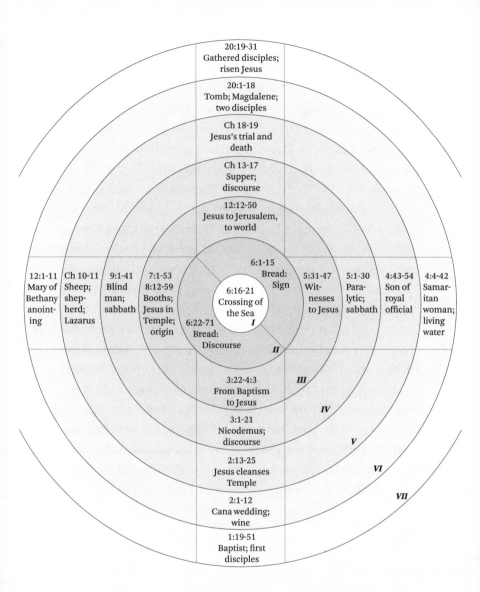

The Gospel of John in Chiastic Form

Adapted from Bruno Barnhart,
The Good Wine: Reading John from the Center
(New York: Paulist Press, 1993), 40.

meaning," or in a scientific metaphor, one can say that the meaning is "an emergent property of the whole." It does not lie in any single part no matter how powerfully configured but in the way the bits and pieces speak to each other, calling each other into resonance. It is detected in the subtlety of the weave and in the energy released in the interplay among the various strands. From the center things, flow out and toward each other, creating combinations sometimes surprising but recognized by the heart as meaningfully congruent. The themes, words, symbols, and images all sound together to reveal hitherto unsuspected dimensions of depth, meaning, and beauty. The validating sense is one of *coherence*, of richly patterned meaning.

One of the most important strands of interplay lies in the counterpoint between the two different kinds of causality themselves: linear and synchronous. It is a completely necessary intertwining; otherwise that great imaginal panorama simply floats out there with nothing to ground it to the marrow of our earthly lives, to feed it with the raw material for the continuous alchemy between the realms. As I said in my earlier chapters, Worlds 24 and 48 are joined at the hip because it is just here—along just this line of interplay—that the great exchange most intensely unfolds. *That* is what our human journey is here, an ongoing dialogue between two types of reality—linear and synchronous; only in the enlightened interplay between them is the true meaning revealed.

The revelation of the larger pattern restores an overall sense of spaciousness and calm. Something, someone, is in charge here; it is not all just random and tragic. The events leading forward in linear time do not cause Jesus's death, and they most certainly do not interpret it; they are simply the necessary unfolding, in linearity, of a deeper purposiveness whose epicenter is already beyond time and whose fullness of meaning can be found only by reading the entire pattern. Like Zacchaeus and Jesus. Like my daughter Lucy on the ferry to the mainland to meet Scott. What we think we are living sequentially in time (with a lot of forward-motion drama and anxiety) is actually already there, all contained in that great stately "now." If we can only find the real center, and the right time scale, then we can begin to actually read the picture.

Babette's Feast

Another striking example of chiastic construction at work, this one perhaps even more deeply cherished by its fans than—dare I say this?—the Johannine narrative itself is *Babette's Feast*. What is it about this movie that audiences find so transfiguring? I believe it is none other than the brilliant radiance of World 12, Christic love in its full plenitude, shining through the tattered veil of our earthly garments and broken hearts. Once again, the deeper meaning is conveyed through the power of chiasm.

The movie is adapted from a short story of same title by Isak Dinesen. In temporal causality, the story unfolds as follows: A sternly devout Christian missionary—a widower with two daughters, Martina and Philippa—has long tended his flock in a small village by the Danish sea. Each daughter in due course falls in love with a man who briefly sets her life on fire, but both relationships wither quickly under Papa's all-pervasive influence, and the daughters quietly resume their posts as his full-time helpers in the mission field. He finally dies, and the daughters, by now middle-aged and with the heart fire long since gone out of them, struggle valiantly to keep the flock together. It is clearly a losing cause.

Arrives on their doorstep one stormy evening a desperate, bedraggled woman, whom the sisters rescue and offer employment as their cook. As the plot unfolds, we learn that she has fled for her life from Paris, where she was once a famous chef before losing everything in the civil uprisings of 1871. She was providentially directed to the sisters' doorstep through the intervention of Achille Papin, the celebrated French opera singer who was briefly the beau of the younger sister.

In one of those extraordinary plot twists, Babette learns that the Parisian lottery ticket she somehow mysteriously still holds has just won her 10,000 francs. She decides then and there to use her entire windfall to cook a proper French dinner for these aging, bickering Danish peasants. The ingredients are ordered and delivered, together with the proper plates, cutlery, wine glasses, and of course the wines themselves. The two primly abstemious sisters watch with growing wonder and horror as their former kitchen servant, who for fourteen years had confined her menus to the requested simple soups and breads, prepares to pull out all the stops and display the full extent of her culinary artistry.

Among the invited dinner guests is the man who was the beau of the other daughter, the once dashing General Löwenhielm—and it is a good thing, because otherwise the dinner party would probably not have made it through the first course! As unaccustomed to abundance as they are to alcohol, the aging disciples are at first suspicious and disengaged. But as the evening wears on and the libations continue to flow, so do the stories . . . and the words of forgiveness . . . and the softening of hearts. At one point in the banquet General Löwenhielm rises and makes a short, moving speech; his eyes briefly meet those of the woman he has always loved, and the tenderness is for a moment almost unbearable. But the moment passes, as all moments do; General Löwenhielm departs, and a short time later the other guests also scatter homeward, pausing briefly en route to join hands around the village well and offer a touching hymn of thanksgiving. Babette cleans up the kitchen and, after a much-savored glass of wine, prepares for business as usual the next day.

What is the point? From the perspective of earth plane causality, it has all been a huge waste. The money is gone, the sweetness brief. But as soon as one applies the chiastic principle, the deeper meaning comes into focus. What has been done has been done in eternity. And there, a nanosecond is all it takes.

The epicenter clearly lies in that short speech, so suffused with healing and grace that it feels itself like a libation poured from the celestial banquet table. Staring straight into the eyes of his beloved, the general begins with a gorgeously appropriate verse from Psalm 85: "Mercy and truth have met together; righteousness and bliss shall kiss one another."[7] Then, in what becomes the film's eloquent climax, he continues:

> Man in his weakness and shortsightedness believes that he must make choices in this life. He trembles at the risk he takes. We do know fear. But no, our choice is of no importance. There comes a time when our eyes are opened, and we come to realize that mercy is infinite. We need only await it with confidence and receive it with gratitude. Mercy imposes no conditions.
>
> And lo! Everything we have chosen has been granted to us. And everything we rejected has also been granted. Yes, we get back even what we rejected. For mercy and truth are met together. Righteousness and bliss shall kiss one another.

There it is! The full imaginal meaning, pouring out through the epicenter. And suddenly the entire picture reconfigures, and the various narrative threads which in linear time had moved jerkily, with many flashbacks, suddenly rearrange themselves in three pristine orbits circulating around this imaginal sun. You can see the results in the illustration on pages 82–83.

In the first ring, revolving tightly around the epicenter and in close dialogue with it, I place the older sister, Martina, and her General Löwenhielm; it is their love story that has carried the World 12 message of this parable. Theirs is a story of quiet fidelity to a heart-knowing beyond all ravages of time. In their brief but timeless reencounter at the banquet table, mortal diamond has become immortal diamond; the imaginal marriage is sealed between them forever.

In the next ring I place the younger sister, Philippa, and her dazzling Achille Papin. It is his fire—*their* fire—and the irrepressible eros and beauty and creativity flowing through their story that channels World 6 and sets the stage for the movie's haunting final line: "Oh, how you will enchant the angels!" These words, first conferred upon Philippa decades earlier by Papin, are now conferred upon Babette by Philippa as the movie's fitting benediction. The demiurgic fire in both of them, at last fully acknowledged, once again glows brightly for all to see.

Finally, in the outer ring, I place Babette's own story of tragic loss and sublime restitution, a perfectly encapsulated image in that already mentioned final vignette when, wine glass in hand, she becomes briefly the Shekinah, "the diffuse shining of God," as Thomas Merton envisions it—Holy Wisdom herself. Merton may well have been imaginally anticipating her when he wrote, "The diffuse shining of God is Hagia Sophia. We call her His 'glory.' In Sophia His power is experienced only as mercy and love."[8]

As both Hagia Sophia and de facto master of revels, Babette

steps seamlessly into the hierophant's role formerly occupied by the old missionary and effects the near-impossible transubstantiation: his small flock finds itself resurrected at the heavenly banquet table, its legs still firmly planted on Danish soil. Particularly in that haunting final image when they gather around the village well (which quickly transposes itself into Jacob's well, the fountain of life), it is clear that all has been washed clean. Again in Merton's words, "Love has overcome. Love is victorious."[9] When viewed through the imaginal lens, the film becomes a shimmering mandala of imaginal abundance and beatitude and a powerful teaching on how fidelity and self-renunciation in this sphere are already icons of that abundance, the broken shards through which the heavenly light pours.[10]

Pondering General Löwenhielm's speech in my book *Mystical Hope*, I wrote:

If only we could understand this more deeply. If only we could see and trust that all our ways of getting there— our courses over time—our good deeds, our evil deeds, our regrets, our compulsive choosings and the fallout from those choosings, our things done and paths never actualized—are quietly held in an exquisite fullness that simply poises in itself, then pours itself out in a single glance of the heart. If we could only glimpse that, even for an instant, then perhaps we would be able to sense the immensity of the love that seeks to meet us at the crossroads of the Now, when we yield ourselves into it.[11]

When I wrote those words back in 2000, I was still taking the first steps toward emerging from the first raw stages of grief over Rafe. Twenty years later they still ring true, perhaps even more so, as I ponder the wreckage of a winter romance so earnestly hoped for but apparently denied. And yet, fundamentally, the imaginal realm is merciful. That is its demeanor and bearing toward us, always. While there is a tendency in secular circles to paint these higher realms as "impersonal" and even morally neutral, the Christian Inner tradition in which my own roots are planted compels me to acknowledge that, as we enter this other causality and encounter what are in fact the tighter tolerances to which the game is played, the more we taste that what is apparently oppositional is not in fact opposition but simply the inevitable friction caused by trying to bend the linear timeline too forcefully to one's own will. As soon as one relaxes spatially and allows the larger picture to fill in, suddenly the mercy reappears, like the full moon from behind the darkened clouds.

The Segments of Babette's Feast in Chronological Order

1 [*prologue*] Introduces Martina, Philippa, and Babette.

2 [*flashback*] The Martina and Lowenhielm story.

    2a Love stirs between them as their eyes meet at the town well.

    2b Lowenhielm becomes a regular at prayer meetings.

    2c Lowenhielm abruptly leaves prayer meeting upon hearing "Mercy and truth are met together; righteousness and bliss shall kiss."

    2d He vows to move on and seek fame and fortune elsewhere.

3 [*flashback*] The Philippa and Papin story.

    3a Papin, smitten by Philippa's singing, offers her voice lessons.

    3b Voice lessons begin, well laced with eros. "Oh, how you will enchant the angels!"

    3c Philippa terminates the lessons.

    3d Papin leaves the village, heartbroken.

4 Babette joins the sisters' household.

    4a Babette arrives bearing letter of introduction from Papin.

    4b Babette establishes her presence in both the kitchen and the mission field.

5 Congregation falls into constant bickering.

6 Babette learns she holds a winning lottery ticket and seeks permission from the sisters to use her windfall to create a real French dinner.

7 Babette leaves on a short provisioning trip.

8 Martina dreams that the feast is demonically inspired.

9 Löwenhielm accepts invitation to attend the feast.

10 Babette prepares and begins to serve the meal. Congregation is silent and suspicious.

11 The feast gradually works its magic.

    11a The congregation gathers and the feast begins.

    11b Martina's and Löwenhielm's eyes meet across the table.

    11c Philippa is unafraid of the feast, surprisingly "in her element."

    11d Congregation slowly mellows.

12 Löwenhielm's speech.

13 Löwenhielm departs, exchanging words of love with Martina.

14 Parishoners gather around the town well for a hymn of fellowship.

15 Babette cleans up the kitchen, savors her moment of triumph.

16 After learning that Babette has spent all her entire lottery proceeds on the feast, Philippa salutes Babette as a fellow artist; "Oh, how you will enchant the angels!"

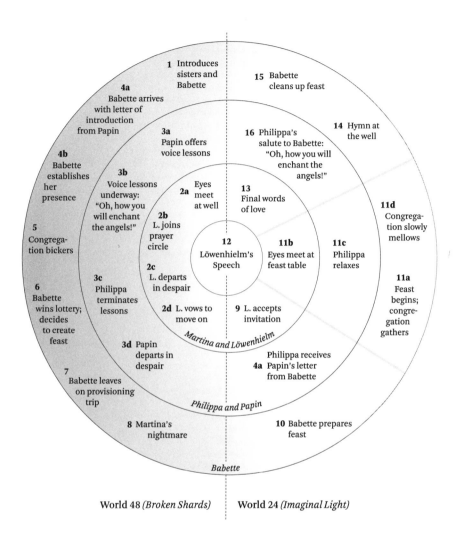

1 Introduces sisters and Babette

4a Babette arrives with letter of introduction from Papin

3a Papin offers voice lessons

4b Babette establishes her presence

3b Voice lessons underway: "Oh, how you will enchant the angels!"

2a Eyes meet at well

2b L. joins prayer circle

5 Congregation bickers

2c L. departs in despair

12 Löwenhielm's Speech

3c Philippa terminates lessons

2d L. vows to move on

9 L. accepts invitation

6 Babette wins lottery; decides to create feast

3d Papin departs in despair

Martina and Löwenhielm

7 Babette leaves on provisioning trip

4a Philippa receives Papin's letter from Babette

Philippa and Papin

8 Martina's nightmare

10 Babette prepares feast

Babette

15 Babette cleans up feast

16 Philippa's salute to Babette: "Oh, how you will enchant the angels!"

14 Hymn at the well

13 Final words of love

11b Eyes meet at feast table

11c Philippa relaxes

11d Congregation slowly mellows

11a Feast begins; congregation gathers

World 48 *(Broken Shards)* | World 24 *(Imaginal Light)*

Babette's Feast in Chiastic Form

Five

THE ART OF
SHAPESHIFTING

So how do you find the center? My World 48 answer is that it's a bit of a learned skill; you learn it by studying the pattern. That's what we were up to in the previous chapter. If you find yourself intrigued by my suggestion that imaginal causality gravitates toward a chiastic presentational mode, you can practice along the lines I've already laid out there: start with completed chiasms where the full pattern is clearly detectible and the work has been done, as in Bruno Barnhart's brilliant exegesis of the Gospel of John or my own first pass at detecting chiasm in *Babette's Feast*. As you work with the completed models, you begin to get some sense of the subtle give-and-take between center and circumference, which constitutes the genius of this art form. The center is that which will allow all the pieces to fall into place in a balanced and harmonious order, revealing hitherto undetected correspondences. You eventually get a feeling for it.

My World 24 answer is that you just *know* it. It does not need to be deduced from a completed pattern; it can already be felt in the bones by a certain quality of its configuration and vibrational intensity. You pick it up like an apple branch in the hand of a dowser that suddenly begins to shake, signaling "Water below!" Like that. It is finally a felt-sense presence that, once grounded and purified, can be caught right in the act, amidst the apparent forward motion of this world. And that, of course, is where the real fun begins.

In this chapter, then, my concern will shift toward learning to spot imaginal causality "in the signs of the times," as they're Biblically known, and as it tugs around the corners of our own lives. You can call it prophecy if you want, but it's really more a matter of finding your way to Teilhard's "naturally advantageous panoramic point." In the previous chapter we explored the overall pattern; here I want to focus in on three of its most important component threads: symbolism, timing, and force. The presence of any one of these elements is enough to set the dowser's branch quaking; the interweaving of all three is a pretty strong sign to get out the shovel and start digging the well.

Symbolism

La Nature est un temple où de vivants piliers
Laissent parfois sortir de confuses paroles;
L'homme y passe à travers des forêts de symboles
Qui l'observent avec des regards familiers.

—CHARLES BAUDELAIRE, "Correspondances"[1]

[Nature is a temple where, from living pillars
confused words sometimes emerge;
Man passes there through forests of symbols
Who look at him with familiar glances.]

(Translation by Cynthia Bourgeault)

The most prominent telltale of imaginal causality is the presence of highly configured pattern and symbolism. We do indeed make our way along the imaginal highway through forests of symbols—"signs and wonders," as the Bible calls them—and as we learn to read them, their glances indeed become strangely familiar.

The biggest challenge on the learning curve, however, is the tendency to place too much emphasis on *individual* signs or symbols. What makes a particular sign or symbol meaningful is that it clearly belongs to a larger pattern from which it ultimately derives its coherence and force. While it may be pushing too far to say that this pattern is always chiasmic, it is *not* pushing too far to say that there is always pattern. I have yet to find an exception to the rule that imaginal causality presents itself in this world not as temporal succession but as spatial pattern, and the faster and more subtly one can grasp the pattern, the more one enters into its modus operandi.

In fact, as you recall from our discussion in chapter 1, the root of the word imaginal is "image," and to the Islamic metaphysicians who originally worked with this teaching, the whole "science of the imagination" lay in learning to read the highly precise and intricate lexicon of visual symbolism in order to make sense of the clues coming so pointedly from worlds beyond. Several centuries later, C. G. Jung circled back to nearly this same idea in his understanding of archetypal imagery, particularly as it plays out in the language of dreams. The hair's-breadth difference between their two interpretations, however, is that for Jung the message seemed to be emanating from a larger and more spacious selfhood on the inner or subjective plane. For those original Islamic metaphysicians, it was emerging from *an objective truth on a higher order of causality.* The "angel of one's being," as this larger archetypal presence was known in Persian Platonism, was never simply a wise inner guide. It was the syzygetic "self" that was already one's *doppelganger*, one's kesdjan selfhood as it is simultaneously playing out in the higher realms. That is why the

Islamic "science of the imagination" could never be about free
invention; it was always and only a rigorous downloading of
the position points in this larger field of reality. No room here
for flights of fancy; only the exact positioning was of cosmic
relevance.

That being said, I would add that in my own experience
imaginal symbolism is verbal at least as much as it is visual,
and while perhaps not given to flights of fancy, it is definitely
playful. Following the classic pattern of the subtle realm,
the symbolic language is fluid, expressive, dreamlike in its
shapeshifting, and endlessly ingenious. It is also a shame-
less punster. I have shared already the story of the "Deep 6"
logo emblazoned on my ill-fated wetsuit, but its sequel is, if
anything, even more hilarious. After my red hat had blown
overboard, Johnny furnished me with a replacement for the
trip home: a baseball cap plucked randomly out of the pile
onboard, sporting the name of one of our local Maine lobster
trap mills. It coyly announced the final verdict on our relationship: "Friendship Trap."

To the extent that one gets really grounded in one's being,
the "*correspondances*" widen still further to include sounds,
scents, colors—the entire canopy of the senses—woven together in a rich, densely concentrated tapestry of cross-ref-
erencing and allusiveness, till at last the shapeshifting itself
becomes the very essence of the imaginal exchange. In one
of my favorite passages in Jacques Lusseyran's *And There Was
Light*, the author describes stumbling as a teenager upon this
insight, which is in fact the linchpin of imaginal causality:
". . . that there is nothing in the world that cannot be replaced
with something else; that sounds and colors are being exchanged endlessly, like the air we breathe and the life it gives
us; that nothing is ever isolated or lost; that everything comes
from God and returns to God along all the roadways of the

world."[2] To know this is truly to have found one's roots and wings in imaginal causality and to begin to taste how those two apparent contrarieties, impermanence and mercy, are in fact a single living stream, fused in this more spacious reality in what Baudelaire calls, a few lines later in his poem, a "ténébreuse et profonde unité"—an obscure and profound unity.

Timing

In this shapeshifting world, time also becomes a vehicle for the expression of meaningful synchronicity and convergence. No longer merely the canvas on which the brush paints, it is itself a powerful brush in the hand of the imaginal artist, contributing actively to the shaping of the overall pattern.

We have seen already how in imaginal causality time is fluid and expressive. That dreadful metronomic regularity of our familiar World 48 suddenly becomes alive and pulsing, taking the outer form of the inner purposiveness it conveys. It can contract down to an instant—as in that General Löwenhielm speech—where the entire meaning of a lifetime's journey of the heart is conveyed in the single glance of an eye. Wave becomes dazzling particle. Or it can expand to cover endless days—years—of dreadful, apparently monotonous repetition. Time takes as long as it takes because in imaginal causality it is a *volume* not a duration. It is always a very secondary expression of intentionality, following like a stern wake wherever the bow is pointed.

Because of the implicitly chiastic structure of the overall pattern, time can also appear to "flow backward," or in other words, events can show up, seemingly out of linear sequence, that will be explained only in the light of events that unfold later. From our linear perspective, this may feel mysterious or even supernatural; words like "prophetic" and "oracular" get applied very easily, and much psychic energy is consumed in trying to decipher the hidden meaning. In reality, the explanation is much more straightforward: it's simply that in imaginal causality there is no "forward" or "backward," only symmetrically balanced parts of a unified whole. To interpret an event seemingly coming out of the future, one has only to locate its counterbalancing element in the completed picture. Then the meaning can be read.

You see this very clearly in Bruno Barnhart's brilliant chiastic reading of the Gospel of John, where in each of the six rings fanning out from the chiastic epicenter, "past" and "future" balance each other and furnish each other's respective interpretive keys. In the outermost ring, the earliest calling of the disciples by the Sea of Galilee is counterbalanced by the last gathering, at that very same spot, where Jesus completes his teaching with the apostolic charge to "feed my sheep." The two illumine and complete each other like a musical call and response. Perhaps even more illuminating is the call and response on Day 6, particularly between the woman at the well (John 4) and Mary Magdalene in the garden on Easter morning (John 20). Taken simply in the linear sequence, this sudden intense exchange between Jesus and an unidentified Samarian woman seems anomalous: how does she know what she knows? Why can she state so clearly the meaning of Jesus's earthly mission when nobody else still even vaguely suspects? And why does Jesus receive her with such deep vulnerability? In the light of the counterbalancing elements in the picture (the marriage at Cana, Mary Magdalene in the garden, the anointing at Bethany) the wider interpretive lens begins to open. These are all fractals of the same timeless whole: the celebration of profound, redemptive feminine love.

The woman at the well is not a prophet; she is an icon of the imaginal fullness. Her meaning becomes clear only in the light of those two later paschal encounters, which round out this sixth day assemblage: the anointing at Bethany and the reunion of the beloveds in the garden on Easter morning. But in the light of that iconic fullness, the deeper meaning of these events comes into radiant clarity. That is how the leveraging of past and future works in imaginal causality.

"To apprehend the point of intersection of the timeless with time is an occupation for the saint," T. S. Eliot once famously remarked.[3] And that is essentially what we are dealing with when we begin to work between the realms. It's not so much that linear time is suspended, but more that imaginal time is always weaving in and out of it, creating its own interpretive counterpoint. Meaningfully configured time is as eloquent as meaningfully configured symbol, and it's in fact what I look for first when I suspect imaginal causality at play. It's not just that events happen, but that they happen exactly *when* they happen in precise and elegant convergences. It's not just that the final leg of Johnny's and my abortive cruise unfolded some random week in March but that I was put ashore on Maundy Thursday, that day of solemn paschal self-searching and surrender. I could read my marching orders well enough. Gradually one learns to pay attention to convergences that emerge, seemingly out of nowhere, with exactly the right timing and force. More often than not they announce the wormhole into a different order of reality.

Force

I spent a good deal of time in chapter 3 trying to reframe the imaginal realm as an active zone of exchange, and where there is exchange, energy is released. Perhaps this could explain the third signature feature of imaginal causality, which is that its pronouncements are not simply interesting revelations for the mind but tend to bear within them the power to *do,* to actually change a situation.

I received my first training in this aspect quite early on from Rafe. "No conscious work is ever wasted," he would insist. No matter how isolated I felt, no matter how much my efforts felt like pebbles tossed into the ocean, if I could simply refocus my consciousness in a more spacious place, the effects of that shift in the inner world would remarkably and swiftly make themselves felt in the outer world. His teaching was as patient and uncompromising as it would be for paper training a puppy. Whenever I got in a bad state, he would leave. Period. As soon as I got myself out of it, he would return. I didn't have to phone him, apologize, or explain; he just *knew.* Sometimes it was virtually instantaneous. No sooner had the inner shift occurred than I would hear the rumble of his old Scout pulling into my driveway. Eventually I learned to trust it.

Sometimes I was on the receiving end as well. There were many times, particularly in those raw weeks immediately after his death, when alone and despairing, I could feel myself sinking into a very deep hole. And then out of nowhere would come that signature wind shift—a small "ping" in the atmosphere, and suddenly I would find myself filling again with hope and resolve—not the result of a deliberation arrived at, but as a totally "new" infusion of energy, like an empty champagne glass suddenly being refilled. That too, I eventually learned to trust. I know there is energy conveyed in imaginal exchange, and that it is nonlocalized, instantly responsive, and damnably efficacious. Some of the popular buzzwords from contemporary quantum physics—*nonlocalized action, morphogenetic fields, quantum entanglement, spiritual generativity*—in fact give us a much better sense of how the mechanics of this transfer actually proceed; it would be fascinating at some point to inquire far more rigorously into the interface zone between quantum mechanics and imaginal causality. I would guess that the correspondences are far closer than we might at first suspect.

It is of course an established datum of imaginal metaphysics that imaginal causality is dominant to our own, producing clear and tangible effects on our own earth plane. The mechanics of how this all works have yet to be fully spelled out, at least to my satisfaction. The traditional and still prevailing assumption seems to be that imaginal causality manifests in the lower realms through the intermediary of human consciousness. It may indeed correspond to "an ontological reality entirely superior to mere possibility," as Jean-Yves Leloup explained it in his *The Gospel of Mary Magdalene* (see endnote 5 in chapter 1), but this ontological reality is realized first on the inner plane as *a shift in consciousness*; then this transformed consciousness rises to transform events on the outer plane. This two-step model is exactly what we saw Walter Wink adopting in chapter 1 when he equated the imaginal realm with the psychic realm, which is for him "the substratum of human existence where the most fundamental changes in consciousness take place." On that basis he could then argue persuasively that "the ascension was a 'fact' on the imaginal plane, not just an assertion of faith" because it "irreversibly altered the nature of the disciples' consciousness." The imaginal intervention furnishes the initial shift in consciousness, then their collectively transformed consciousness does the job of rearranging the pieces in World 48.

It is hard to argue against this position. This is exactly what Rafe was talking about when he said, "No conscious work is ever wasted." Transformed consciousness is a profound viaduct of radial energy, and it does indeed generate an energetic field around itself in which a whole different order of causality holds sway. Transforming our own minds is always the place where we can begin to work, and as we work, the outer effects will sooner or later make themselves known.

Still, I am a bit reluctant to pin the whole transmission chain on an obligatory intermediary of human consciousness. My own experience is that imaginal causality has its own intrinsic purposiveness and can make its intentions clearly known even without the direct conscription of our conscious assent. The whole Jonah syndrome was evidence enough of the diabolical brilliance of this artistry when it's aimed against you. Metal sheared, headwinds raged, electrical systems failed: it was clear from the outset that the Greek and I were making our way within a very disturbed energy field, and I am reluctant to conclude that we were the sole generators of it. I am no scientist, but I suspect strongly that these currents are electromagnetic in nature, and that electromagnetic energy is the actual chief operative in imaginal transmission—not simply "human consciousness," which is in this context way too imprecise a description. While our specific individual pixel of consciousness (itself electromagnetic in nature) can certainly impact significantly upon the total energy field, it neither creates it nor in the end disarms it; that help must emerge from considerably further up the Ray of Creation.

I say this partly to try to recapture the imaginal from any effort to portray its domain as simply an interior plane of human consciousness—an exclusively "upper left" phenomenon, in Ken Wilber terminology. The old Islamic masters—and Gurdjieff—were quite correct in insisting that objective means *objective*, not simply an inner (subjective) truth acted out on the outer plane as a "psychic fact." Imaginal causality possesses intelligence, agency, truthfulness, and its own legitimate ways and means of carrying out its purposes here in these lower realms. And those purposes, as we have seen, are ultimately cosmic and collective, involving the vital exchange between the realms of nutrients which, no matter how subtle, are in fact *substantial.* They actually exist. The exchange is real. It is important not to forget this.

Surprise

If there is a common denominator in the characteristics we have thus far explored—pattern, playfulness, energy, timing, force, wind shift—I would say it lies impressionistically in the quality of *surprise.* Whenever I become aware of imaginal causality at play in a situation, I am also distinctly aware that it does not arise from entirely within myself. It *enters.* It is not the final step in a pedantic process of weighing and sifting but the sudden infusion of something new; something not thought of before, a fractal of a larger cohering pattern, which itself bears and confers the energy of that larger pattern. Over and over again, it is that sudden "ping" of something new entering that wakes me up, shifts my state, and summons Rafe and his old Scout back to my driveway.

Often these imaginal interventions will appear to emerge from out of left field: a "chance" acquaintance or invitation that appears at exactly the right time, a series of coincidences, a symbolism too highly configured to disregard. *Babette's Feast* is woven precisely out of these "coincidences," but the causality is far from accidental. In the larger chiastic picture a coincidence is not a coincidence at all but a primary compositional technique through which the imaginal tapestry is woven.

People often ask me if I'm talking here about what Gurdjieff calls "third force," that mysterious X factor (or third line of action) that must enter a situation to break the impasse and create genuine new arising. In one sense yes, I believe that imaginal causality often—perhaps even typically—manifests in our gridlock-ridden lower world as third force. But we need to proceed cautiously here, merely noting resonance rather than leaping to "same as" conclusions. At best, third force is merely one *expression* of imaginal causality, not a full synonym for it. Nor is everything that breaks up an impasse in our immediate world an expression of imaginal causality; chance and accident abound here as well. We have to look at the deeper purposiveness and read the larger pattern.

The same goes for another question I am frequently asked: is imaginal causality the same as what Christians call grace? In a fundamental sense I believe this is true: the core experience in both is that there is an infusion of something that was not palpably present before, something of a higher order of compassion and plenitude that radically shifts the outcome in our external world. But if we are going to proceed in this direction, we need to avoid falling into two traps. First, we have to stop identifying grace with a happy outcome. The imaginal is not unresponsive to our deepest desires, but neither is it easily swayed by sentimentality or our own limited sense of what is "right and just." Its mercy always reflects the big picture, and just as there is tough love, so also is there tough grace.

Second, we need to wean ourselves away from viewing grace as a rare or exceptional intervention. In this respect, I believe that the imaginal metaphysics we have been exploring in this book offer Christians a whole new window of insight into one of our tradition's most beautiful intuitive treasures. For in the light of imaginal causality we can see clearly why grace is never an exception to the rule; *it is rather, simply, the law of the higher causality playing out in this lower one.* It is cosmically "normal," and it can become a steady state—in fact, many (including Gurdjieff and Jesus himself) regarded it as the normal and necessary state for proper human functioning within the wider cosmic exchange. It can indeed become a place you come from, not a thing that happens to you. But for grace to become *that* real and *that* operative, it must finally draw you over the line into its bailiwick—and for that to happen, there is a journey of purification to be undertaken. As the Quaker mystic Thomas Kelly wrote, "Those bright shoots of everlastingness can become a steady light within if we are deadly in earnest in our dedication to the Light and are willing to pass out of first stages into maturer religious living."[4] That metamorphosis will be the subject of our next chapter.

Trope

A SCHOOL FOR
THE LORD'S SERVICE

PERHAPS YOU THINK I have learned these things about imaginal causality through a scholarly immersion in esoteric teachings, and to some extent that is true. But I would say that the foundations were already well laid down in me by my years of ad hoc formation in Benedictine monasticism. When St. Benedict set out in the sixth century to establish what he called "a school for the Lord's service," two of the most important pillars of his curriculum were in fact a direct training ground in the art of imaginal causality.

The first of these pillars is the underlying Benedictine rhythm itself, grounded in that slow, steady alternation of *ora et labora*—"pray and work"—orchestrated on the backbone of the Divine Office. Seven times a day—and once more deep in the night—the monks step out of the linear stream to pause, reflect, and collectively offer up their prayer, chiefly through chanted or spoken psalmody. The ancient words of these small offices, themselves emanating from thousands of years ago, reverberate against the tempos of the monastic day, furnishing a de facto grid for learning "to apprehend the point of intersection of the timeless with time."

And of course, the symbols and images themselves begin to resonate—Baudelaire's "forêts des symboles" comes alive and starts vibrating with night sounds, furnishing a whole new interpretive lens as one's life becomes progressively more interwoven and magical. Synchronicities begin to crop up with predictable regularity between the psalm texts chanted in the office and the events in the daily rounds, as one slowly gets a sense of one's life playing out in the deeper hand of God. I will never forget the bitterly cold December day at St. Benedict's Monastery, high in the Colorado Rockies, when, after struggling for hours with a broken hose in the pump house, I finally got the thing fixed, switched on the pump, watched the pressure gauge slowly climb, and suddenly heard myself break into the advent canticle we had sung at Lauds early that morning: "With joy you will draw water from the fountain of salvation." Where did *that* come from? But that "where" is exactly the deeper transformational wisdom at work here. On the surface, the Divine Office may appear to be merely an ornate specimen of medieval devotional piety. Beneath the surface, it is rigorous training in learning how to live one's life under the conscious sway of imaginal causality. Part of my purpose in writing this present book is to call to wider attention this "beneath the surface" (or mesoteric) aspect of the Benedictine tradition and to show you how to engage it more fully by accessing it through the practices of conscious awakening we have been exploring here.

The imaginal training becomes even more systematic when we move to that other great pillar of the Benedictine transformational program, *lectio divina*, or "sacred reading." The practice entails a slow, prayerful reading of a scriptural text, in which periods of active reflection and inquiry alternate with times of spontaneous prayer and contemplative stillness. It is the backbone of Benedictine scriptural exegesis, and it is currently enjoying something of a renaissance as the Christian contemplative awakening continues to gain momentum.

What many contemporary practitioners do not yet fully recognize, however, is that in the classic Benedictine pedagogy,

lectio was never simply "Bible study"; it was a systematic training of the unitive imagination—or in other words, the capacity
to begin to read the imaginal landscape. It proceeded according to successive levels, which in the early centuries varied in
number and order but eventually settled down to a four-tier
model, widely known as the "four senses of scripture."

The first sense is the *literal* level, which corresponds to the
causality of linear time. It's all about facts and figures: what
happened when? Who influenced whom? Is it fact or fiction?
It's the causality of World 48, and it's the inevitable starting
point. But then comes the remarkable second step, as the aspiring monk moves beyond reading chronologically and begins to read *christologically*, with all stories, signs, and symbols
pointing directly to Christ. In other words, our monk is being
trained to think *chiastically*—and as we have seen already, this
is the watershed that must be crossed in order to enter the
sphere of imaginal causality. It was through his years of monastic training in lectio divina that Bruno Barnhart was able to
grasp the chiastic pattern so profoundly in the Gospel of John,
and his *Good Wine* heralds the welcome return of a form of
Biblical exegesis—essentially, imaginal exegesis—which was
eclipsed by the scholasticism of the thirteenth century and
has not been seen since, either in church or university.

But there are still two more levels. At the third—the *allegorical*—level, the Christological training wheels drop away as
one begins to process the whole of life according to imaginal
causality, with one's own heart furnishing the new epicenter.
This is the step that Jung enshrined so powerfully in his teachings on the archetypal imagination. To a heart so attuned, the
scriptural passages suddenly light up with profoundly configured meaning. I remember the story my teacher Thomas
Keating frequently told about discovering as a young monk
that the Old Testament story of the Exodus was powerfully

his own story, his own symbolic journey out of the captivity of Egypt. "It was like seeing my life flash before my eyes," he exclaimed rather excitedly. I felt the same way when I realized that the Jonah story, formerly dismissed as a "quaint" folktale, suddenly furnished the working script for my winter's sailing adventure. The allegorical level is like that. Once you can read imaginal causality directly, the chiasm of your own life opens up like a book, and Holy Scripture is still one of its most potent exegetical tools.

But there is yet one more step awaiting: the *unitive* or *anagogical* stage. At this level, one's personal life story ceases to be a treasure house to be mined and is seen for what it is: simply a fractal of the one great heart of our Common Father, which beats throughout this entire vast Megalocosmos, and in which all things find their alpha and omega. This is the level of understanding hinted at in those great Pauline visions of a universe in which all things are "put under the subjection of Christ"—i.e., within the cosmic, universal ordering—and in which Christ yields himself back into the Father "so that God will be all in all" (1 Cor. 15:28). It is a vision stunning in its grandeur and its humility, and it anticipates the future toward which we may be collectively hurtling and which Paul, perched on that "naturally advantageous panoramic point" was already intuiting.

Little did I suspect in my early attraction to Benedictine monasticism that I was actually entering a system that would introduce me to imaginal systematics. Certainly this would be news to most people, not only outside the Benedictine tradition but within it as well! Still, when one approaches the Benedictine phenomenon from the perspective of imaginal causality, the whole thing makes perfect sense. For as St. Benedict, an otherwise obscure monk, somehow intuited fifteen centuries ago, only by obtaining full imaginal fluency could his "school for the Lord's service," i.e., in active partnership with the conscious circle of humanity, actually deliver the goods. The institution he brought into being is Christianity's oldest ongoing school of imaginal formation, and it is still its most brilliant.

Six

IMAGINAL
PURIFICATION

IN THE PAST two chapters we've been looking at some of the ways in which imaginal causality expresses itself in this world. Now it's time to look a bit more closely at some of the ways in which this expression can be distorted—or in other words, areas in which some purification of the vehicle is necessary in order to ensure a greater reliability and consistency of connection.

The Sufis call this work "polishing the mirror" or "cleansing the lens of perception." For Christian readers long accustomed to associating purification with sorrow and penance, this "housecleaning" metaphor may indeed offer a refreshing new take. In this more praxis-oriented context, the issue is not so much remorse for our moral failings (although that never drops out of the picture) as it is a deliberate effort to keep the viewing screen clear so that what falls on it is not immediately distorted by lower-order agendas.

The biggest single area of distortion lies in the tendency to drag the interpretation down to the level of magical thinking. At this level the focus is on individual "signs and wonders," almost invariably drawn from the stock repertory. An eagle feather drops in your path, a rainbow appears in the sky, a shooting star streaks across the night sky, and suddenly you are in receipt of a personal message from God! Or perhaps you race on ahead and start filling in the pieces of the imaginal puzzle with your own imagination and mental calculations. Then you are in some ways worse off than if you had never begun, conscripted to a scenario that exists only in your own head. In both cases there is a *level confusion* going on here, and this confusion is what will inevitably switch the message (however accurate it may have been at its initial point of impact) onto a generally unreliable track.

Who is this "I" who is receiving the message? The confusion is between two levels of consciousness, which in the classic typologies of both East and West are known as "psychic" and "subtle."[1] The bottom line is that imaginal causality belongs to the subtle level of consciousness; all attempts to capture it at the psychic level will lead to distortion—at best innocuous, at worst downright dangerous.

The psychic level of consciousness is that intermediate state at which a growing sensitization to transpersonal (a.k.a. "psychic") phenomena is still firmly tied to an egoic (or narrative) self-center. It is the next rung above rational consciousness on the early Ken Wilber maps,[1] and insofar as it does signal the initial opening of the imaginal capacities, it represents progress. But it is a very unstable place in the growth curve, and until the tension is ironed out a lot of damage can be done.

I will speak only in passing here of those more dangerous levels of magic and the occult, which happen in exactly this configuration at its extreme negative pole, i.e., a pronounced psychic capacity tied to a strong, amoral personal will. With concentrated attention and training, it is indeed possible to draw down the energy of World 24 and even World 6 to wreak havoc on this earth plane. Gurdjieff called such people "hasnamusses,"[2] but perhaps the old term *evil* will serve just as well. We see them in the Hitlers, the Jim Joneses, the cult leaders run amuck, and in many more who wreak harm in a much more subtle but pervasive way (I would personally place Ayn Rand in that category): too much psychic power, too little love. The moral inversion at work here is not only an affront to the image of our common humanity, it also badly misinterprets the nature of the higher energy itself, which appears under this filter to be simply an impersonal, amoral, "spirit in third person,"[3] another mechanistic force to be harnessed— *not*, as it really is, a powerfully compassionate and coherent relational field bearing the moral heart of God. When Teilhard de Chardin insisted adamantly toward the end of his life that "God is a person, God is person," he was not picturing an old man with a beard up in the sky. He was saying, rather, that as we proceed further and further into those luminous spheres, we encounter more and more fully the personal, radiant, tender, and intimate presence of the divine heart, which can never be relegated to an "it." It is always a "thou," and it pulls us inevitably toward greater thou-ness, the ultimate sacrifice that is love's.

The imaginal realm properly corresponds to the subtle level of consciousness, which in turn corresponds to a different kind of selfhood. We move here necessarily from a narrative or egoic seat of selfhood to the beginnings of authentic witnessing selfhood. The concept is not well understood in Christian spiritual theology, which still tends to confuse the mythical beast of "true self" with the high egoic functioning of World 48. Witnessing selfhood is a World 24 phenomenon. That discrete sense of a personal "I" marching along a linear timeline held in place by memory and desire, gradually shifts to a larger and more unboundaried selfhood, the "wave" form of oneself, as it were.

Paying attention not to what you are but to *that* you are is how the anonymous medieval author of *The Cloud of Unknowing* summarized this fundamental shift in perspective.[4] For Gurdjieff, this would be the beginning of the transition from "essence" to "Real I." I have written extensively about this transition elsewhere, most recently in my book *The Heart of Centering Prayer*, so I will not elaborate further here.[5] But I would want to make very clear, with regard to our present concern, that *imaginal causality can only be reliably read beginning at the level of witnessing selfhood and sooner or later demands that one join it at that level.* The cost of admission to this new and more intense bandwidth of reality is ultimately your phenomenal self. Those things that you once *thought* were you—your history, your emotions, your particularities, your "descriptions" (as Beatrice Bruteau calls them)[6] are precisely those things offered into the refiner's fires in order to create a being that can reliably listen and respond.

Seeing with the Eye of the Heart

In the Western Inner traditions there is a strong implicit thread that this shift to a new seat of selfhood is inextricably linked to a *new operating system* of perception, centered in the heart. "Blessed are the pure of heart, for they shall see God," said Jesus, in these words of the sixth beatitude inaugurating not only a new pathway of purification but in fact a new phenomenology of it. The heart is already implicitly identified as the seat of imaginal vision, and as the teaching gets fleshed out over the centuries, particularly in mystical Sufism, the consensus continues to build that the heart (rather than the cognitive mind, i.e., the brain) is the true organ of spiritual perception and the seat of our imaginal selfhood. In Kabir Helminski's cogent summary of traditional Sufi teaching on the heart, *Living Presence*, you will certainly notice several capacities already specifically underscored in the previous chapter as foundational to imaginal literacy, including the capacity to read pattern, visual and verbal symbolism, overall unity, and nonlinear timing:

> We have subtle subconscious faculties we are not using. Beyond the limited analytic intellect lies a vast realm of mind that includes psychic and extra-sensory abilities, intuition; wisdom, a sense of unity, aesthetic, qualitative and creative faculties; and image-forming and symbolic capacities. Though these capacities are many, they are operating best when they are in concert. They comprise a mind, moreover, in spontaneous connection to the cosmic mind. This total mind we call heart.[7]

The teachings of Christian East follow a parallel track, with an increasing emphasis on a quality known as *attention of the heart* as the required prerequisite for following Christ directly into World 24—"putting on the mind of Christ" in the more familiar Pauline language. The eleventh-century Orthodox teacher Symeon the New Theologian precociously recognized that this mind of Christ actually emerged from a significantly higher level of consciousness than we humans can normally sustain; without the mediating presence of this inner attention, he bluntly claimed, it is flatly impossible to live the gospel teaching:

> In a word, he who does not have attention in himself and does not guard his mind cannot become pure in heart and so cannot see God. He who does not have attention in himself cannot be poor in spirit, cannot weep and be

contrite, nor be gentle and meek, nor hunger and thirst after righteousness, nor be merciful or a peacemaker, nor suffer persecution for righteousness sake.[8]

The goal of "putting the mind in the heart" gradually came to dominate the transformational program of these Eastern Orthodox Hesychasts. The phrase shows up more and more frequently in the writings of *The Philokalia*, that great compendium of Orthodox mystical Wisdom, and as it does so, the lineaments of a practice begin to reveal themselves. Part of this practice entailed an actual energetic training (always taught one-on-one, to prepared students only) in learning to concentrate attention in the region of the chest. The lion's share of the preparatory work, however, lay in the struggle with the "passions": those turbulent, self-referential emotions that will always obscure the viewing platform and drag our sense of selfhood back into the gravitational field of the lower realms. The practice, Symeon claims—his own variation on the universal spiritual theme of nonattachment—is actually quite simple, though of course, not easy:

> You should observe three things before all else: freedom from all cares, not only about bad and vain but even about good things . . . your conscience should be clear so that it denounces you in nothing, and you should have a complete absence of passionate attachment so that your thought inclines to nothing worldly. Keep your attention within yourself—not in your head, but in your heart.[9]

If this sounds more than a little unpalatable, like deliberately squandering our God-given human right to "go for the gusto," remember the context in which we are raising this possibility—*which world do you want to play in?* The fact remains that from the standpoint of imaginal causality, the energy consumed maintaining the nucleated egoic selfhood (with its constantly whirling orbit of stories and emotions) as the seat of identity drains energy and drags one back into the denser gravitational field of World 48 and below. Break that bond, and the energy is immediately released back into one's being as that additional boost required for participation in World 24 causality. Maurice Nicoll aptly reminds us that our capacity to see is state dependent: "As your being increases, your receptivity to higher meaning increases."[10] This is essentially what Rafe was trying to teach me when he would promptly depart whenever I fell into a negative state. From the perspective of World 48, it sounds quite "unsupportive," but I had come to him essentially petitioning for a novitiate in World 24, and that's what he intended to deliver. The inconvenient truth remains: If you are going to play in World 24, all those heavy, negative emotions you are clinging to and wallowing in are useless. They belong to the density of that other realm. You can indulge them as much as you want there as you perfect your World 48 self. But to step fully across the line into the imaginal realm, there can be no more wallowing or clinging; it's transforming all the way.

Consistency

The second hurdle in this steeplechase of purification is the demand for consistency. You cannot play in both worlds—or rather, you can, but you have to play according to the laws of the higher causality. Any attempts to "colonize" the imaginal as a place you visit for your personal enjoyment or spiritual storytelling is ultimately a cul-de-sac—again, a level confusion.

You activate your imaginal citizenship by walking the path persistently and consistently. How you get there is where you'll arrive.

Once again, Rafe was all over this particular teaching. It was one of the most distinctive traits of his mode of seeking. As soon as he *saw* something, he put it immediately into action, letting the chips fall where they may. "I think that people who love each other wind up trapping each other," he observed one sunny August day as we shared a cup of cappuccino on my deck. Then BAM!, two days before Christmas, he announced he would be spending Christmas alone in his hermitage, in part at least to clear out some of those little relational rituals that were already starting to silt in between us. "Can't I at least come up and visit?" I wheedled. "What if you don't and see what happens next?" He was always the empiricist, testing and measuring. He allowed no gap between idea and its execution. And he was right.

That gap has always been my particular bête noire on this path. Because I come endowed with a particularly creative and agile mind, I can easily get lost inside my Prospero's castle and wind up missing the objective demand to *act* on what I know. It lives in me as a truth on the inner plane only, not in the concrete choices I actually make in the world; there is a split there, a "buffer," as Gurdjieff called it. And alas, this misguided notion that it's possible to have one's cake and eat it too—to be an aficionado of the imaginal while still living completely in the comfort zone of World 48—essentially turns the spiritual journey into a glorified game of trivial pursuit. This perhaps all-too-human failing, known less charitably as "insincerity," has dogged the path not only of countless individuals but of institutional Christianity itself and is probably the single greatest energy leach on its otherwise extraordinary message.

As Meister Eckhart once observed, "There are plenty to follow our Lord half-way, but not the other half."[11]

The Lord is patient; he does not smite. But as Thomas Keating once famously remarked, "the two of you play ring-around-the-rosy for a while." On a playing field where all else has been equalized, progress in the imaginal realm is logged in direct proportion to how well one learns not only to apprehend but actually to *follow* the path as it increasingly presents itself to your inner understanding. One of those cardinal laws of World 24, fully operative in these lands here below although almost universally unrecognized, is that *means and ends must coincide*; otherwise an action self-cancels in World 24. Which means that it self-cancels here as well; firestorm though it may appear to be, its impact will quickly fade.

Out of the Depths

We now turn to the question of *obedience*. To our modern ears the term seems to suggest knuckling under to an external authority, but the Latin root of the word—*ob-audire*—actually means to "listen deeply" or "listen from the depths," "with the ear of the heart," as St. Benedict puts it. And yes, that listening is, in and of itself, also a doing, a *submission* to what the heart has heard.

In his *Meditations on the Tarot* Valentin Tomberg vividly pictures this spiritual positioning in terms of the Hanged Man, the twelfth major arcanum of the tarot deck. On the card the man is literally upside down. His feet are in the air, symbolically higher, more able to hear and respond to that "gravitation from above" (or in other words, imaginal causality), whose steady drumbeat is detectible only to the heart. It is by walking in obedience to that deeper listening—rather than by thinking, calculating, reflecting—that one actually responds and follows, actually begins to walk the path. The feet, the moving center, get it before the mind does.

By way of illustration, Tomberg cites the prophet Abraham, who hears the Lord's voice commanding him to "Go from your country and your kindred and your father's house to the land that I will show you, and I will make you a great nation." (Gen. 12:1). He doesn't yet understand the "I will make you a great nation" part of the instructions (that will unfold in time), but he does understand "Go." He begins walking.

I can certainly validate the truth of this story in my own life. The decisions made in response to that inner emanation from the heart have the nature of being effortless. They literally fall like ripe fruit from one's branches. When the invitation to go to Colorado and work with Rafe opened up, no decision was ever made. I simply quit my job, packed the car, and left.

Of course, the sticky wicket here is that this paradigm itself can all too easily get coopted into simply another form of magical thinking. The real operational challenge is that most of us in the early stages of the journey do not yet have the capacity to discern accurately the level from which an inner impulse is emerging. Gurdjieff speaks to this dilemma in a fascinating teaching about what he calls "A, B, and C influences." At first, when attention of the heart has not yet stabilized, we are pulled by every impulse that crosses our radar screen; we cannot distinguish reliably between the random play of attraction and fancy (A influences) and invitations emerging from that higher imaginal plane (B influences). In particular, there is a terrible trompe l'oeil, for a long, long time in the journey, between the distinctively different timbres of the lower passional self—the *nafs* in Sufism, or "soul" in the common parlance of our day—and the authentic homing beacon of the heart. The squeaky wheel gets the oil, and the nafs drama will initially tend to drown out the subtler vibration of that other channel. But with practice, as that heart presence is strengthened through the twofold disciplines of attention and surrender, we begin to develop a qualitative *level* of discrimination—we can distinguish, as Grace Cathedral's dean Alan Jones once quipped, "between what's essential and what's merely interesting." We follow, our feet leading more confidently. And at some point, as a critical threshold is crossed, something crystallizes inside us that will finally stay put. The imaginal sonar kicks in fully, and we call to ourselves a C-influence teacher with the same effortless force as Zacchaeus up his sycamore tree. Because something has finally quickened in us that can live above the ceaseless push/pull of this world, we are at last real players in the game. At which point, the ring-around-the-rosy comes to an end and the journey begins in earnest.

The Law of Fate and the Law of Accident

I will never forget the stark comment made by Canadian spiritual teacher John de Ruiter at a teaching I attended many years ago, that the higher spiritual realms do not get more relaxed and permissive as we ascend. Instead, they are drawn to tighter and tighter tolerances.

Gurdjieff would most likely have concurred with this assessment and had his own characteristically vivid way of picturing it. The lower realms, he taught, are under the Law of Accident. "Shit happens," as the common parlance goes, and there are no great consequences, for when all is said and done, it's only A influences cancelling other A influences, irritating but basically innocuous. As Jacob Boehme once bleakly observed, "It is all only a useless carving in the great laboriousness of man. . . . What good builds up, evil breaks down; and what evil builds up, good breaks down."[12] And thus things indeed seem to be ordered in this world here below, the randomness of it all screened from our sight only by our insistence on imposing a pattern. The good side of it is that very little of real demonic import gets permanently engendered here either; the sea is just too choppy.[13]

At the gateway of the imaginal, however, one comes under a whole different order of causality, which Gurdjieff called the Law of Fate. *Fatum*, or fate, remember, is the name given on the classic Great Chain of Being map to the realm just above ours, typically associated with the planets. But while in the popular imagination fate may suggest astrological charts and soothsaying, *fatum*, in fact, stands on the other side of a fundamental causal watershed; the coin of the realm here is no longer A influences, but B influences. We are beyond the random perturbations that comprise our experience of causality down here in "the lower forty-eight." And since we are dealing with a realm that is causally dominant with respect to our own, a higher level of precision and tighter tolerances must necessarily pertain. Coloring outside the lines is permitted under the Law of Accident; not so under the Law of Fate. Higher standards across the board are required in consistency, obedience, clarity, sincerity—not only for one's own safety, but for the safeguarding of the whole cosmic equilibrium. More power is wielded here, and of a kind that at its upper limits transcends even the imaginal sphere of influence and begins to link directly to the properly causal realms. Mistakes here are more costly.

Looking back on my winter odyssey, I would now say that this is the ballpark where things went wrong. I didn't take seriously enough the post I was occupying or the energy flowing through it. Folks would sometimes comment that there was a certain energetic force running through my teaching—a *transmission*—but I tended to dismiss these comments as

New Age hype. I did not feel myself to be particularly forceful or accountable but simply, as I mentioned earlier, the cabin boy left temporarily in charge of steering the schooner after its captain vanished overboard. I certainly did not feel myself to be under the Law of Fate.

And probably this is true; alone I almost certainly am not. But to the extent that I continue in imaginal partnership with Rafe—and on his end the consistency, obedience, clarity, and force wielded are growing in quantum leaps—I am at least under some obligation to crack the whip. Permission was neither asked nor granted to let go of the towrope and slide gracefully toward the shore. That was something I did not know about myself before, or did not take with sufficient seriousness. Now I do.

Trope

PUTTING IT
ALL TOGETHER

IF YOU FEEL drawn to work with a situation according to imaginal causality, where (and how) do you begin? As we near the end of this section of the book, let me see if I can draw the whole picture together in the form of a few basic guidelines. Over the years I've found these particularly helpful for keeping my own work on course.

1. First of all, never underestimate the "sacred sobriety of common sense," as Rafe used to call it. If a situation can be easily dealt with according to the laws of World 48, by all means start there. You don't need a faith healer for a headache; you just take some aspirin.

2. Try, as a matter of principle, to avoid all World 96 thinking. Gurdjieff called this level "formatory thinking." It's the world of recycled opinions, slogans, broad generalizations, and rigidly behavioristic psychological models. Labeling, typing, group think, political correctness: all those modes of prepackaged discourse will lock your mind into familiar rut tracks leading nowhere. If you're going to think, then *think*. Use your own mind, heart, and grounded presence to see what is actually going on and to try to understand with what is the most awake in you, not the most asleep.

3. The tip-off as to whether imaginal processing is really indicated lies in the presence (or absence) of those markers we've already been looking at over the past several chapters: highly configured symbolic or imagistic patterns, synchronicities that seem actually to belong to a larger pattern, and time functioning as an active compositional element, not merely a backdrop. Generally, I'd say at least two markers should be present; not to test the degree of its "imaginality" (just like you can't be a little bit pregnant, a situation can't be a little bit imaginal), but rather, to keep your own itchy fingers under control. Don't jump the gun; wait and see what arises. Eliminate other options first (as discussed in point 1), and consider the strength of your own interior fortitude. Because once you start to walk down this path, you will need to be committed to seeing it through.

4. When you actually start working with imaginal causality, the most helpful "user's guide" I've found—believe it or not—is that single, sublimely challenging sentence in the middle of St. Paul's great discourse on love in 1 Corinthians 13: "Love bears all things, believes all things, hopes all things, endures all things." It's the second item—believes all things—that really delivers the punch. This does not mean to refuse to face up to the truth, but rather, that there is a higher and a lower way of perceiving and acting in every circumstance of life. One way leads to cynicism and a closing off of possibility, and the other way leads to higher faith and love and a more fruitful outcome. To "believe all things" means to orient yourself toward the highest possible outcome and strive for its actualization.

That was the watershed decision I had to make

concerning Rafe nearly twenty-five years ago: do I process his death according to World 48 or according to World 24? All around me the psychological and traditional spiritual models were unanimously advocating closure, "grief work," "letting go," "getting on with my life." Something inside me said to keep walking toward him, and I did—straight into the imaginal where the fruits have more than validated the risk.

It's a delicate balance, of course, and finding the right touch with it is part of the learning curve. On the one hand, there needs to be openness to the valid input coming from World 48, and to the processing of psychological and developmental issues that appropriately belong to that realm. The imaginal is no place for spiritual bypassing. On the other hand, one must not forget the teaching already laid out, that you can't play in two worlds at once—or if you do, it has ultimately to be according to the laws of the higher. There's a certain knack required for learning to assimilate the shadow graciously and honestly, yet still keep walking toward the light.

5. Finally, I've found that the single biggest developmental challenge when learning the ways of imaginal causality is the tendency to take over and carry on with one's own imagination. Something is received, something genuinely known, but then the mind gets playing with it and starts to fill in the details, so that before long the originally pristine imaginal seeing has run off its own rails and been recaptured in World 48 as fantasy and expectation. The imaginal is always going to arrive with an element of surprise. If you've already written the script, it's no longer imaginal causality.

There is a learner's curve here, for sure, but part of this "seeing it then losing it" is built right into the path itself, part of the inherent challenge of living at the intersection of two worlds. You're in the groove for a while, then you fall out of it. But as those two sturdier containers slowly grow within you that will allow you to authentically hold the tension—*impartiality* (i.e., non-identification with a preferred outcome) and *patience*—things gradually get better. The purification practices we have been looking at in the past two chapters will help build the stability of those containers, but all roads eventually lead to a mysterious waiting in emptiness, the painful but requisite final step. The heart will always know what it wants, deep inside, and does not need to be reminded. Do not use your mind to create scenarios for your heart. When the time is right, the heart's own speaking will be clear.

Seven

WHAT ARE WE HERE FOR?

IN MY CITATION several times now of key excerpts from William Segal's essay "The Force of Attention," I have repeatedly called attention to his comment, "Without the upward transmission of energies through the medium of conscious attention, the world would give in to entropy." But I have so far deliberately sidestepped the sentence that directly precedes this assertion and is in fact essential to its interpretation.

The full paragraph (the next-to-the-last in the essay) actually reads as follows:

> Attention is not only mediating; it is transmitting. Giving and receiving, God speaks to man. Receiving and giving, man speaks to God. *Just as man's structure needs to be vivified by the infusion of finer vibrations, those very same vibrations require the mixing of coarse material for their maintenance.* Without the upward transmission of energies through the intermediary of conscious attention, the universe would give in to entropy. In man, the smallest deformation of a balanced attention closes down this two way communication.[1]

I have called out the critical sentence in italics because now is the time to address it directly. What is this "coarse material" that is somehow needed for the maintenance of the cosmic equilibrium, and what is our part in furnishing it? And note that by "our" I am not speaking in this case simply about us human beings, but "our" in the sense of the lower realms themselves. What part does "coarseness" play in maintaining the Ray of Creation? Why is *mi*, our beloved *mixtus orbis*, not simply a cosmic folly or illusion, but a vital player in the whole unfolding?

This question needs to be settled before we can move on to consider the conscious circle of humanity, for without some sense of the authentic worth and purpose of this earth realm in the cosmic scheme of things, it is very difficult to fathom the amount of excruciatingly tender care exerted on our be-half, or to tap into those deeper motivations of the heart that would draw us to take up our post not out of duty or enlight-ened self-interest, but out of an authentic wish to "lighten the sorrow of our Common Father."

Axial religion—the term now commonly used to designate the great efflorescence of spiritual breakthrough and insight that sprang up worldwide in a remarkably compressed time period between roughly 800 and 200 BCE[2]—is generally weak on this point. Across the sweep of the great sacred traditions (with the notable exception, perhaps, of shamanism) we en-counter a pervasive sense that "here is not home." Whether you call it exile, fall, or illusion (the three prevailing assump-tions in the combined metaphysics of East and West), there is a deep unease about this condition of embodiment and a general assumption that coarseness is itself an impediment to the full attainment of the enlightened state. That should prob-ably be stated much more strongly: not only *an* impediment, but *the* impediment, the chief roadblock. On the maps of con-sciousness we have been exploring, "coarse" (a.k.a. "gross") is always at the bottom, and given the overall Neoplatonic skew of axial metaphysics, there is an almost inevitable tendency to equate density with a "fallen" condition. "Gross" in the physical sense—roundly corpuscular—quickly melds into "gross" in the emotional sense—vile and repulsive. My own teaching in these pages has of course drawn on many of the traditional metaphors (ladder of ascent, Great Chain of Being) reflecting these built-in biases; it is virtually impossible to enter the metaphysical conversation without them.

But is this *really* an illusion, this beautiful, fragile constructal zone we briefly inhabit and water with our tears? Christianity in its finer moments intuited that there might be more to the story—"For God so loved the world that he gave his only son," in the venerable words of John 3:16. At its epicenter it carries an unquenchable certitude that something goes on here of such inestimable worth that even the formless Infinite would be *compelled* to take form—"make himself an element," in Teilhard's rendition[3]—in order to uphold and sanctify this preciousness on its own terms. But this totally on-target mystical intuition could never fight its way upstream against the flood tide of world-hating and body-denying metaphysics that surged out to meet it. More fundamentally, the problem was— and remains to this day—that from within the metaphysical givens at hand, it was impossible to say why that love was so tendered in the first place. So the question was sidestepped. "Giving his Son" became instead the consummate demonstration of the preeminent divine agape, and our human role was simply to adore and obey.

Gurdjieff made a heroic beginning at a new metaphysical paradigm in which something can actually be *seen*. Although few of his admirers have had the gumption to wade into those spiraling hydrogen chains portraying the ostensible biochemistry of the Trogoautoegocrat, his model can at least be applauded for what it is: a brilliant attempt to demonstrate on an *empirical and material* basis what contribution our *mixtus orbis* makes to the greater cosmic equilibrium. From behind all the intricate detail there emerges an overall picture of the biosphere—organic life on earth—as itself a crucial stabilizing and mitigating influence in the overall planetary harmony. The "coarse material" is our own organic existence here in this tiny corner of the Megalocosmos, and what it contributes (whether by conscious donation or involuntary reappropriation) is a vital part in the overall homeostasis that allows anything to be in the first place. Gurdjieff's sweeping vision of a single, intricately interwoven cosmic "self-specifying system" in which everything has its unique role to play still seems to me a far stronger vehicle for the arousing of genuine human conscience than the standard theological models emphasizing the total self-sufficiency of God and the essentially gratuitous nature of our human existence here.

My own response will again return us to theological language—though hopefully not to a replay of those same old scripts. I want to begin directly with the question itself: What part does "coarseness" play in the overall dynamism of manifestation? What does it contribute to the mix that would be missing or inexpressible without it? And if you will permit me, I would like to ease into this question by way of a story. It's actually a picture as much as it is a story, a picture burned onto my heart during a rather extraordinary fifteen minutes in a concert I attended many years ago.

I had gone that afternoon with a friend to hear the de Pasquale String Quartet offer an all-Beethoven program at the Delaware Art Museum. These brothers four—William (first violin), Robert (second violin), Joseph (viola), and Francis (cello)—were all respectively first chairs in the Philadelphia Orchestra, or in other words, some of the finest string players in the world. They were clearly about to put their mastery to the test, for included on the program was the formidable Opus 132. This exquisite late quartet, one of Beethoven's final works, boasts a third movement that is virtually unplayable. For something approaching fifteen minutes it simply shimmers like the full moon on the ocean, gradually building intensity but along a path so subtle as to be almost beyond the reaches of human artistry. Almost inevitably, an aspiring quartet will either play the movement too "yang," trampling over it like an eighteen-wheeler on a golf course, or too "yin," losing the subtle inner momentum so that the whole thing turns to mush.

Three minutes into the movement it became electrifyingly clear that they were going to nail it. They were exactly in the groove, riding the razor's edge with an apparently effortless intensity. As the momentum steadily built, audience and players fused into a single stream of crystalline attention. The energy in the room was electric; the excitement became more and more palpable.

Curiously, however, as the energy mounted, the de Pasquale brothers seemed to get quieter and quieter, contracting into a kind of laser-like stillness. No emotion showed on their faces, not a single extraneous gesture—only the soft play of their hands on the bowstrings and an occasional blink of an eye. They had literally "melted" before the music, with only the backbone of their bare presence and their years of cumulative experience to draw down lightning from the sky. I did not know at the time exactly what I was witnessing, but I could feel its force already working in me. Little did I know that the musical icon they became for me in that timeless few moments would in turn become one of the cornerstones of my own theological understanding.

I believe, fundamentally that *that's* what we contribute; what the gift of coarseness contributes. Holy denying. Second force. Gravitas. The backbone of form that draws down the lightning from heaven. Light is said to be dark in outer space until it strikes an object; perhaps that's what finitude furnishes. The grace of materiality is that it allows something to *materialize*, i.e., to come into existence and self-expression, to contribute its own unique mode of being to that great single outspeaking of the name of God.

"I was a hidden treasure and I longed to be known, so I created the worlds visible and invisible" is how one of the great mystical sayings of the Islamic Hadith Qudsi pictures the primordial divine yearning for intimacy and self-disclosure that got the whole cosmogonic ball rolling in the first place. Each world along the Great Chain of Being is not merely the next step in a mathematical progression; it is a specific set of conditions that allows for the expression of some very specific aspect of the divine heart. And in fact, the word *cosmos* in the original Greek actually means "ornament." If rather than seeing these worlds as beads on a chain we saw them as balls on a Christmas tree, we might better understand how each of these precious cosmoses is beautifully and uniquely artificed to bring forth some specific aspect of the divine longing to be known. The chain links drop out, and you stand like a small child on Christmas Eve, bedazzled by the wonder of it all.

So let's explore a bit further the contribution of this particular ball called *mi*, or *mixtus orbis*. We know that these forty-eight laws by which our plane of existence is ostensibly governed make for a fairly dense set of constructal givens that most of us find reasonably irritating much of the time. But the deeper burden we bear may well be the pervasive, haunting sense that we are indeed playing in two worlds at once, the two of them in almost constant tension. There is blessing here, but it is also a cross that we bear. That great wise woman Helen Luke says: "Wholeness is born of the acceptance of the conflict of human and divine in the individual psyche,"[4] thereby acknowledging that the conflict does indeed exist, the one we spend so much of our lives repressing, masking, outrunning. Not only the saints among us but the sinners as well find ourselves pinioned at "the intersection of the timeless and time," our infinite yearnings trapped inside our finite bodies. It's this irreducible sense of twoness that may indeed drive those original axial metaphors for "exile" and "fall." The constriction is not an easy condition to work within.

But what if there is no mistake? No fall? What if this frustrating arrangement furnishes exactly the right conditions for the expression of something that can be expressed in no other way? Suppose there is some quintessence of the divine heart that can reveal itself only under these conditions, only when thus tensioned, like a cello string pegged between heaven and earth? And if so, what might this quintessence be?

What if it is love?

Well, that's not how we were taught to think about it, is it? "God is love" is almost the first thing you learn in Sunday school, furnishing the complete and sufficient explanation for the created order. From the effulgence of divine love the visible world comes forth, imperfectly reflecting a quality that already exists in divine perfection. But if seven decades of living into the Christian Mystery have brought me anything, it is the growing clarity that love is not the alpha; it is the omega. The agape love that nearly universally is assumed to be the starting point for creation is not in fact the starting point. It is the fruit of a long transformative journey whose eye of the needle is right here, sitting squarely on that *mi-fa* shock point.

The mystics, of course, have long intuited that something like this might be the case. I have spoken already about Boehme's brilliant intuition that "the impressure of nothingness into something" is not accomplished without, like

Odysseus, engaging the Scylla of constriction and the Charybdis of desire. In those first primordial stirrings by which the "Endless Unity" brings himself into "divisibility and perceptivity," there is no effulgence of agape; there is only constriction, compression, and craving. The Endless Unity begins its journey into form by a fundamental self-tensioning, compacting the only "raw material" as yet at hand—the divine will—into a "magnetical hunger"[5] (which is at that point insatiable since nothing as yet exists on which to slake it) so that a current begins to arise within the Divine Unity that will eventually draw all things toward the whirlpool of being. The current thereby generated, streaming out into World 6 as the fundamental creative force, is not agape but eros, the pure creative fire of attraction and desire. Mystics of all ages have felt this erotic force churning and pulsing through the entire cosmos, not only as its enlivening passion but as its basic structural principle.[6] But this is not yet the deepest and most mature realization of love itself. It is not yet that most intimate laying bare of what lies hidden in the divine heart.

The "coarse material" contributed for this transfiguration of eros is our own finitude. Only when love enters the constructal givens of this world and encounters the constrictions of choice, finality, separation, tragedy, betrayal, and heartbreak do its most tender and exquisite facets begin to emerge—qualities such as steadfastness, tenderness, commitment, forbearance, fidelity, and forgiveness. These mature and subtle flavors of love make no sense in a world where everything simply flows. They are cured on the rack of time—and at that, only in the awakened human heart willing to consciously bear the conditions as intentional suffering. $A = ek$ is my own alchemical formula for this, where a = agape, e = eros, and k is the kenotically surrendered heart. (Kenosis, of course, is the

Greek term used by St. Paul in his celebrated hymn in Philippians 2:5–11 to convey the radical nonclinging that comprises the very essence of the mind of Christ.)[7] When that depth of surrender is laid before the surging force of eros, then the inexpressible music begins to sound.

Is it simply another one of those imaginal felicities that the name de Pasquale means "paschal?" For of course this same alchemical formula is at the heart of that one great mystery for which "God so loved the world that he gave his only son." Yes, of course there were other options. "Do you think I cannot appeal to my Father, and he will at once send me more than twelve legions of angels?" says Jesus as the soldiers come to arrest him in the garden at Gethsemane. But then the eye of the needle would be sidestepped. If here in the density of World 48 is exactly the place where the quintessence of the elixir of agape is to be extracted, then the conditions must not be overridden but rather *lined*—with the grace of that flowing, higher luminosity, lined with World 24, so to speak—so that the crucible of transformation can be endured here, so that it does not break our spirits. That is for me the imaginal meaning of the paschal mystery. Our Common Father really does love this world, because it is here that the restless roving and churning of that sea of eros comes to rest, and we hear in the silence the still, small voice of love.

This is also for me the real charter of the conscious circle of humanity. We are called to work back and forth across the divide of finitude not because the conditions here at the denser level are false, but because they are *hard*. Help is needed here, and it is freely and gratefully given. Because what we give back here, though miniscule and always, I suppose, clumsily offered, is indeed that "hidden treasure" for whose sake the entire created order came into being.

Apprivoiser

What would the Ray of Creation look like if redrawn in chiastic form with agape as its epicenter, as in the diagram on page 133? Let me comment briefly on a few of the perhaps surprising symmetries highlighted in this new visual arrangement. First, notice how the inner circle—*mi* (World 48) and *sol* (World 12) orbit around the imaginal epicenter at *fa* (World 24). The three of these collectively comprise the *sphere of the personal*, whose chief function in the great Trogoautoegocrat is the generation and maintenance of agape, transmuted from the raw, demiurgic force of eros. In earlier chapters I have already identified this sphere with the mystical body of Christ.

The value of the personal realms has perhaps not been sufficiently appreciated in traditionally hierarchical metaphysical maps in which they appear to form an intermediate zone between insentience and the higher realizations awaiting in the presumably impersonal bandwidths. In terms of the overall cosmic equilibrium, however, and particularly of the *divine* self-realization of which we have already spoken (i.e., "I was a hidden treasure and I longed to be known"), moving the personal realms to the chiastic center makes an all-important point about the real teleology at work here. Whatever is manifested at the center sphere is what ultimately brings the entire structure into balance.

In Saint-Exupéry's beloved *Little Prince* there is a wonderful exchange on the subject of *apprivoiser*. The term is not quite translatable into English. "To tame" is the usual translation, but it does not mean "domesticate" (there's another word for that). Rather, *apprivoiser* brings overlapping connotations of gentling, caring for, and creating a sense of specialness. "When you tame something, you form ties," the fox explains to the little prince; then he adds the powerful clincher: "Tu

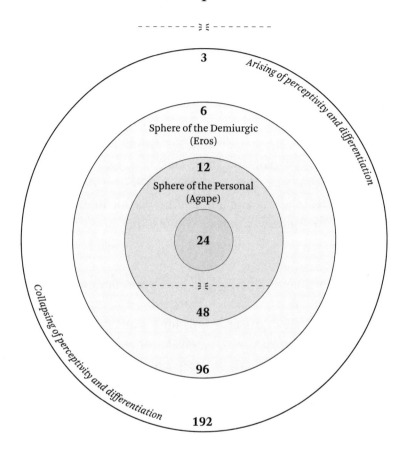

1

3   *Arising of perceptivity and differentiation*

6

Sphere of the Demiurgic
(Eros)

12

Sphere of the Personal
(Agape)

24

48

Collapsing of perceptivity and differentiation

96

192

The Ray of Creation in Chiastic Form

deviens responsable pour toujours de ce que tu as apprivoisé."
(You become responsible forever for everything you have
tamed.[8])

By analogy, then, this inner circle is the place where raw
eros is apprivoisé, and what emerges are those gentler flavors of caring, tenderness, and particularity generated in and
through the act of caring. The impact of this tempering zone
is felt throughout the entire chiasm—which means, of course,
along the entire Ray of Creation. But its influence is now no
longer merely provisional; it is pivotal.

Saint-Exupéry's fellow Frenchman, Teilhard de Chardin,
is, I believe, intuiting along much these same lines when he
writes in *The Human Phenomenon* one of his most moving reflections:

> So many times art, poetry and even philosophy have de-
> picted life as a woman, blindfolded, tramping down a
> dust of crushed existences. In life's profusion we find
> the first traces of this apparent hardheartedness. Like
> Tolstoy's grasshoppers, life passes over a bridge of accu-
> mulated corpses. . . . Life is more real than lives, it has
> been said. . . .
>
> Insofar as the general movement of life becomes more
> ordered, in spite of periodic resumptions of the offensive,
> the conflict tends to resolve itself. Yet it is cruelly recog-
> nizable right to the end. Only from the spirit, where it
> reaches its *felt* paroxysm, will the antinomy clear and the
> world's indifference to its elements be transformed into
> an immense solicitude—in the sphere of the person.[9]

Again we find the same intuitive recognition: that the realm
of the personal—particularly when it comes to maturity in
the fully awakened and surrendered human heart—is at the

epicenter of some fundamental cosmogonic process. As we move outward through the concentric rings of our diagram, we can picture vividly what this process looks like. Worlds 6 and 96 now counterbalance, comprising a larger (but more primitive) domain in which untransformed eros holds sway and sheer generativity is the order of the day.[10] At the next ring out, Worlds 3 and 192 also counterbalance, with World 3 heralding the first arising of perceptivity and divisibility out of the primordial anguish, and World 192 marking the return to that primordial anguish as separability collapses back into infinitely dense unity.

Ultimately, the whole chiasm floats in World 1: the endless, unknowable, uncreated abyss that both mystics and astrophysicists mostly now see as the steady state of a cosmos too vast to comprehend with either mind or heart.

A tiny oasis in a fathomless sea, to be sure. But it is on the basis of the inner circle generated around *fa* (itself fulfilling that basic Law of Three stipulation, "The higher blends with the lower in order to activate the middle") that I stake my claim that the imaginal realm is the true epicenter of the Christian Mystery.

Personal Transformation in a World Where Everything Belongs

I have already mentioned Helen Luke's piercing observation that "wholeness is born of the acceptance of the conflict of human and divine in the individual psyche." If my premise is correct that what goes on here in this challenging dance between the realms is exactly as it has to be for the fulfillment of greater cosmic purposes, this also fundamentally shifts the way I understand the relationship between my World 24 self and my World 48 self. If it's a dance, both partners are needed.

In my explorations of spiritual practice in this book, I have so far been preaching mostly the hardcore transformational wisdom of the nondual paths: imaginal transformation requires a transcendence of the narrative or phenomenal self as the seat of my selfhood. And I stand by this teaching. The crossing of that *mi-fa* threshold—and certainly full participation in the conscious circle—requires a stabilization of the witnessing self. The narrative self is a product of World 48 causality *only* and has neither motility nor permanent identity beyond the limits of its immediate constructal zone. A hard truth to hear, perhaps, but better to hear it now than later.

In the light of the model we have been considering here, however, I think it is possible to say something about the relationship between these two parts of our selfhood that is often not noticed in traditional spiritual psychologies. In those traditional models, the work before us is often looked at as a "dismantling" of the phenomenal personality, often tellingly called "the false self" (easier to dismantle something you've already labeled as false). The age-old antinomy between true self/false self, old man/new man (St. Paul), ego/Self has more than polarized the transformational turf into "spiritual warfare." Once again, this is a level confusion. By design these two selves live within us, for they are the amphibious vehicle expressly needed for navigating the imaginal intertidal zone. In right relationship, they will assist us in our real human task, which is to weave Worlds 24 and 48 into a single flowing "kingdom of heaven."

Gurdjieff's take on the subject is, as usual, unique. He too draws an initial distinction between those two very different aspects of our selfhood, which he calls "essence" and "personality." Essence is what we are born with; personality is what we acquire through education and cultural conditioning. It is manifestly in that sense "not us," and mistaking the culturally created simulacrum for the real thing is the first and perhaps most serious mistake of our human journey. Unless we awaken to the mistake and take vigorous measures to correct it, we will simply float through our days in a dream of ourselves.

But his next step is unexpected. Rather than merely echoing the familiar chorus that the personality must be dismantled, he argues instead that it is the necessary "food" for the *growing* of essence.[11] For Gurdjieff, there is no return to a supposed primordial "true self," and "essence" is not yet "Real I." *Nor, in the lack of this active contribution from the personality, will essence grow.* It is by venturing out, learning the skills, developing the agency, and taking the risk that we enter the transformative process that will eventually deliver "Real I" as its imaginal fruit. A person who is rich in essence but has not developed a strong vehicle for its expression in this world is, in Gurdjieff's terms, a "stupid saint." The courage to take that outbound tack and become a real player in World 48 is utterly necessary if we are to put ourselves, as the de Pasquale brothers did that day, in full service to that inexpressibly more beautiful music that wants to sound on our fragile human bows.

This means that we do not "outgrow" our phenomenal self. As long as we are in this bodily life, it is our instrument, the violin we will play to make the celestial music sound. We will speak through it, act out of it, care for it, and do our best to keep it in playable condition. The oppositional stance is quite unnecessary, quite unproductive. Integrative work at the psychological level is a necessary and ongoing task of good stewardship, in order to keep the baseline at least at World 48. The only thing that changes, once witnessing selfhood is attained, is that *that's* where we now mostly live; the phenomenal self has lost its allure as the presumed seat of our being.

Recognized at last for what it is, a precious and serviceable tool—like a violin in the hands of a de Pasquale—it is set free to do its thing as brilliantly, passionately, and particularly as only a finite self can.

And the hidden treasure is finally known.

Eight

THE
CONSCIOUS CIRCLE
OF HUMANITY

THERE'S AN OLD piece of Hasidic folklore that claims that our world at any point in time is held in its planetary orbit by thirty-six conscious human beings. They don't know each other, and they don't even know if they're among the thirty-six. But the quality of their work, rising like incense into the earth's atmosphere, creates around our fragile planet a sturdy bandwidth of protection, blessing, and guidance.

That's the gist of the notion of the conscious circle of humanity, as Rafe absorbed it from his readings in Gurdjieff and passed it on to me. The notion absolutely galvanized him. He returned to it again and again in our conversations, both as the endpoint of his striving and the explanation for the fierce urgency of his quest. It was also the lens through which he approached our own relationship and tried to make sense of what the two of us were up to. He yearned for full membership in this circle, and I think he made it. Otherwise, none of what I've been writing about in these pages would ever have come to pass.

Like so much of what Rafe knew, his version of the conscious circle is a bit of an amalgam: the Gurdjieffian teaching passed through the filter of his own mystical intuition. Gurdjieffian purists may be horrified. But it's the path as Rafe understood it, formed me in it, and continued to walk it unswervingly after his physical death. It's the path as we mutually threshed it out during our human time together and continue to explore and articulate together during this phase of our work, the give-and-take between us as strong and flowing as ever.[1] Since his vision is now essentially mine to carry (as mine is his), and since we will no doubt spend the rest of our lives, in whatever worlds they ultimately play out, ground-truthing each other's heading, let me simply follow on here in the direction in which we pointed each other.

Essentially, the conscious circle is an intense zone of imaginal interchange in which advanced beings on both sides of the form/formless divide—i.e., some still in their physical bodies, others no longer so—join hands across the realms for a mutual exchange of wisdom, tempering, blessing, protection, and occasional course correction. You might look at it as a kind of "bodhisattva bandwidth," in which the best of our human altruism is met and matched from the other side by a sincere compassion for our human predicament and the skillful means to help. This is the circle of "ye watchers and ye holy ones" (as the old hymn goes), antiphonally proclaiming their mutual commitment to protect, uphold, and bring to completion all that has been set in motion here.

The whole notion is by nature evolutionary, incarnational, and collective. Membership in the conscious circle of humanity is not about bailing out of our earthly responsibilities to seek personal enlightenment in more spiritualized realms. It fits squarely within the Gurdjieffian notion of *reciprocal feeding*; in fact, only within this framework can its purpose really be understood. We have seen now how each realm along the Ray of Creation furnishes a specific and unique set of conventions that is both valid in its own right and essential to the dynamic equilibrium of the whole. Our earth plane is real, substantial, and good, and it has a pivotal role to play in the cosmic transmission chain. But it is vulnerable as well, subject to falling back into the gravitational field of the lower realms (Worlds 96 and 192) and hence losing its clarity as the individual note *mi* through which the crucial *mi-fa* shock must pass in order for the upward and downward transformation along the Ray of Creation to proceed undisturbed. Our *mixtus orbis* requires active support in order to be able to hold the note it is required to sound; on its own, the tuning always falls slightly flat.

The conscious circle of humanity, then, is essentially a realm of service, as a bodhisattva bandwidth must necessarily be. Even as one steps forward to receive its greatest gift, which I have ironically come to think of as "temporary permanent individuality" (more on that to follow in the next chapter), it is in full recognition that this "gift" is not a reward, but simply the necessary vehicle through which the work is done here. It is bestowed impartially, and in the way such gifts always are at this level of cosmic responsibility: for collective service, not for personal attainment. To aspire to and win a place in this circle is never an attainment—or if so, only for the most spiritually naïve. It is a deeper and more binding form of service.

Note that I am not talking here about the angelic realm, although in our common, sentimentalized notion of things you might initially have that impression. In our Hallmark greeting card version of the larger cosmic life, angels are often depicted as personal servants, swooping to our aid to find our lost car keys or prevent personal harm. This is a fundamental misunderstanding of the angelic realm in the first place, which is really the *causal* realm—World 6, three worlds above our own—whose chief work lies in overseeing the fundamental logoic architecture of creation itself. This is most certainly not the realm of personal spiritual concierge service, and it is in any case not the level that the teaching under consideration is operating on. Personal, relational, and supremely *this*-world oriented, the conscious circle of humanity bears the classic hallmarks of an imaginal world phenomenon, and it is indeed solidly within the imaginal bandwidth that this circle situates itself.[2]

Wisdom Schools

It may not be the angelic domain, but the conscious circle *is*, supremely, the domain of Wisdom. Indeed, right here in this bodhisattva bandwidth is where the great lineage of Wisdom schools flows through the history of civilization like an underground river, mostly hidden from sight but coming to the surface as needed to provide course corrections and necessary guidance. Gurdjieff's *Beelzebub's Tales to His Grandson* offers a fascinating microhistory of these schools, tracing the Wisdom river from its original upwelling on the lost continent of Atlantis, through those "wise beings" of Egypt and Babylon, to the tragic history of the mysterious Ashiata Shiemash, whose brilliant but short-lived program for rebooting human conscience forms the chiastic epicenter of Gurdjieff's entire sprawling masterpiece. There are allusions as well to schools in Tibet and in Central Asia, and it is clear that Gurdjieff's own sense of mission is framed within this greater flowing of the Wisdom lineage.

While many of Gurdjieff's details are deliberately fancified, the schools he mentions are by and large familiar, some through legend, others through historical record. The schools of Atlantis, Egypt, Babylon, Chaldea, Pythagoras, Parmenides,

Zoroaster, and Tibet are all well documented by historians and cross-referenced by some of the most sacred texts of the world's spiritual traditions, including our own Old Testament. Once you get used to looking for them, it's striking to watch the pivotal cross-pollination between these schools and the emerging Israelite nation. Somewhere around 1700 BCE a famine lands the young Semitic tribesman Joseph in Egypt, where he is soon fully immersed in the most powerful Wisdom school in recorded human history—and it is in fact, literally, "out of Egypt" two centuries later that the nation of Israel is born. Then, six centuries beyond that, the capture of Israel by the Babylonians and subsequent forty years of exile lands Israel once again in the precincts of the most powerful Wisdom school of its day, from which it returns with the "newfangled" notions of heaven and hell, the angelic world, individual salvation, and a first glimmer of the "son of man" (or bodhisattva) archetype dawning on the horizon of consciousness.

Widening the viewing screen still further, we can see that Israel's collective leap to a new level of consciousness under this Babylonian Wisdom sojourn is simply part of a still larger explosion by then well underway worldwide, ushering in what is now widely known as "the first axial age." In a remarkably compressed time period (800–200 BCE) we watch the individual firecrackers popping off all around the planet—Lao Tzu, the Buddha, Zoroaster, the Old Testament Wisdom literature, Pythagoras—announcing a new era of collective awakening as humankind emerges from tribal consciousness into a rising sense of individual destiny and personal responsibility.

The emergence of this global "first axial" shift offers a textbook example of conscious-circle intervention in the affairs of our earth plane. In line with those stipulations laid out on page 140, it is *evolutionary* (oriented toward a quantum leap in planetary consciousness), *incarnational* (working with real human beings through the historical events of the times) and *collective* (involving the synergy of the group). Over the ages Wisdom schools seem to have emerged as the favored "shop front" for conscious-circle activity, and while the Wisdom river is always flowing, the schools themselves tend to come above ground either in times of planetary crisis or on the threshold of a new evolutionary leap in consciousness, when the planetary homeostasis is temporarily destabilized and thus particularly vulnerable. In the language of contemporary chaos theory, they emerge predictably in those zones of "local instability," not only because that is where change is possible but because that is also where local change will have the maximum global effect.[3]

Our own era clearly qualifies on both counts. We find ourselves situated on the edge of what many are now calling "the second axial awakening," heralding a quantum collective leap toward the next level of conscious evolution. At the same time we face the radical destabilization of our planetary ecosystem—already well underway through global warming—and the collapse of cultural institutions that have carried us in the West for more than two millennia. From the point of view of the great Trogoautoegocrat, Western civilization is perhaps expendable, but the biosphere certainly is not. We will either make the leap to the next level of conscious evolution—the so-called "integral" level or capacity to think from the whole—or we will wipe out a good part of a planetary legacy millions of years in the making and in the process put the entire Ray of Creation at risk. And at such critical junction points, the vigorous intervention of the conscious circle of humanity is not only a possibility; it is a virtual certainty. In the words of General Löwenhielm, we need only to "await it with confidence and receive it with gratitude."

The Work of the Conscious Circle

Here in World 48 we tend to think of consciousness-shifting initiatives in terms of "think tanks," convocations, websites, political action, and task forces. The conscious circle does not work that way. It is an imaginal phenomenon through and through, which means that it operates according to the laws of World 24. This means, from our earth perspective, that its influence is more subtle and *indirect*. Although it really isn't indirect at all; it simply works directly at the psychic or radial-energy level: shifting energy fields, removing psychic toxins, sweetening the planetary atmosphere, and directly purifying the inner body of the outer world. As mentioned in chapter 5, its modalities are better described in the language of modern physics than of classical theology. *Nonlocalized action, morphogenetic fields, quantum entanglement, open systems, chaos theory*: all of these terms point toward a delivery system that is diffusive, holographic, and synchronous, i.e., not subject to linear causality. And while Teilhard cautions that the universe touched at this level will not outwardly change its characteristics—it will only become "more supple, more fully animate"[4]—in point of fact, the outward pieces can and do get rearranged, not so much by a direct override of the causality of World 48 as by a skillful use of timing and psychic force to shift the basic configuration of the playing field.

In general, from whichever side of the divide one participates in the conscious circle, and whether the work is carried out alone or in a group, there are three main lines of work within the overall job description of "keeping a watchful eye over the cosmos" (as the Gospel of Thomas puts it): "cosmic dialysis," guidance, and occasional direct delivery of third force. Let's consider each of these in turn.

Cosmic Dialysis

Dialysis, of course, is the purification of a system that cannot purify itself. We encounter it in our familiar world mostly in the form of malfunctioning kidneys. But it offers a very good analogy for the primary and ongoing work of the conscious circle: the regular monitoring and cleansing of our planetary psycho-energetic atmosphere so that it remains habitable for sentient beings and is able to play its part in the greater cosmic exchange.

Much of this cleansing work has to do with the removal of the toxins generated by fear, greed, violence, vengeance, and shame: the stench of World 192. As we have seen already, actions in the outer world are always accompanied by an inner energy signature. When we pave over pastureland to build shopping malls, not only are we removing essential nutrients from the biosphere, we are also filling the noosphere (Teilhard's term for this surrounding psycho-energetic field) with the psychic toxin of greed. Entitlement, indifference, groupthink, mass hysteria, addiction, violence, even the isolation and suspicion that hang like a heavy pall over affluent, gated communities—all of these create serious toxicity, real imaginal pollution, which rains back down on our planet in the contagion of cancers and autoimmune diseases. The main ongoing work of the conscious circle is to reduce this psychic smog, and where possible to rebalance it with a direct infusion of those other elements, which we have been referring to as "fruits of the spirit," namely love, joy, peace, patience, goodness, faithfulness, gentleness, and self-control. These, too, are powerful psycho-energetic nutrients for both noosphere and biosphere; in fact, in their absence human habitation quickly becomes untenable.

Traditionally much of this has been the deep, solitary work

of those symbolic "anonymous thirty-six": the hermits and small communities of religious adepts who quietly, faithfully lift up the world in their intercessory prayer. In a beautiful reflection in her book *Old Age* Helen Luke explains that the Latin *intercedere* actually means "yielded between," and the hermit in intercessory prayer is literally "yielded between heaven and earth"—which is exactly the positioning of the conscious circle of humanity.[5] From there, this solitary work flows out to join all other work at that same vibrational level according to the principle that physicists call "quantum entanglement," and Rafe called "no conscious work is ever wasted."

The spiritual practice of *tonglen,* perfected to a high art in Tibetan Buddhism but known in some form or another in all the sacred traditions (in Christianity, the basic art form is called "substituted love") is a particularly direct application of this basic intercessory model. It entails the conscious and voluntary ingestion, on the in-breath, of the toxicity of a painful situation or disease, allowing the toxicity to be transmuted in one's impartial and compassionate heart, then releasing it on the out-breath in the form of healing and blessing. This is cosmic dialysis at its most literal and efficacious, and it is the fundamental work of the conscious circle of humanity.

Sometimes the assignment becomes more proactive, however; the invitation is extended to actually create a missing element. This is the alchemy we saw so powerfully unfolding in the movie *Babette's Feast.* As her own heart looked deep into the hearts of those bickering and dispirited peasants, Babette could see that what they were really starving for was the experience of unconditional abundance; until that hunger had been satisfied in them—"pressed down, flowing over" (Luke 6:38)—they would be unable to actually access the spiritual teaching they professed to believe in. That was the missing imaginal nutrient she set out to generate directly in her lavish, over-the-top banquet. No sermons, no guilting, no "How could you have forgotten your teacher?" Just a simple, compassionate marking of the missing ingredient, like any good cook, and then an imaginative reshuffling of the ingredients suddenly miraculously at hand (somehow they always are) in order to meet the lack. The work is joyous, and when you begin to see its results, richly satisfying and far more efficient than the constant chiding and moral exhortations that make up so much of the tedium of World 48.

Often the work goes on sideways; the *real* missing element emerges almost as a byproduct when one's conscious intention is focused on something else. The ecumenical monastic community at Taizé, founded in the immediate aftermath of World War II, set out to establish itself as a center for spiritual reconciliation and harmony, and it has done very good work here. But what Taizé will be remembered for long after the political initiatives have been forgotten is the body of song that emerged virtually spontaneously as the community reached out to the world's youth. The songs are of such harmonic purity and healing beauty that they actually put into the atmosphere the elements they invoke: trust, hope, light. I personally believe that Taizé chant qualifies as what Gurdjieff would call "objective art"—art coming from a higher plane of consciousness for specific cosmic rebalancing purposes—and that the "downloading" of it in this remarkably imaginal spiritual community is a vintage example of a conscious-circle tag team at work.

Sometimes the alchemy is deliberately and fiercely intentional. My final example here is of this latter type. Over the past ten years it has been my privilege to offer annual Wisdom schools on Holy Isle, a tiny island off the coast of the Isle of Arran in the Inner Hebrides. The island has a long spiritual history going back to the Celtic seafaring monks, but its most recent history has been written by the Tibetan Buddhists, under the visionary leadership of Lama Yeshe Losal Rinpoche, who bought the island in 1992 through his Rokpa Trust and set out to transform it into not only a microcosm but a *transmitting station* of universal peace, ecological harmony, and clarity. To do so required establishing a particularly high vibrational purity, which the community has remarkably managed to generate and maintain. On the human energetics side this plays out in a very high moral code that retreatants and day-trippers agree to be bound by when they come here: no intoxicants, no violence, no theft, no lying, and no lustful or abusive sex. On the natural side, the island has been gradually stripped of invasive species and returned to a natural habitat where native species of ponies and sheep wander freely among the humans, each gentled by the presence of the other. It is a high-vibrational, essentially celibate purity being generated here, like a concertmaster's perfect 440, which the entire orchestra tunes to. One can sense the concentric circles of this crystalline vibration radiating out into the world, calling things back into harmony around a master tuning fork that had gone missing in all the cacophony. It is marvelous, directly vibrational conscious-circle work, of the kind I expect we will be seeing much more of in the days to come. Needless to say, teaching here is like rolling off a log; in the clarity of this atmosphere, thinking goes easily, problems are solved, and concepts almost too complex to fathom are grasped like child's play.

Guidance

One of the most important functions of the conscious circle is to read "the signs of the times." We have seen already how this capacity actually belongs to the imaginal level of perception; it is not attainable under the laws of World 48 for all one's mental brilliance because it is not linear but *spatial*, a direct seeing from that "naturally advantageous viewing point." The baseline requirement for individual participation in this imaginal seeing is the capacity to maintain, or as quickly as possible to restore one's consciousness to a level where such spacious vision is possible. And in practical fact, not only in *Beelzebub's Tales* but throughout sacred tradition as a whole, the preparation to receive any prophetic revelation classically entails a period of rigorous inner purification so as to bring the body/mind into a state of total, alert readiness. Gurdjieff's mythological Ashiata Shiemash with his elaborate 120-day preparatory ritual of fasting, prayer, and self-mortification[6] is mirrored in the strivings of innumerable desert solitaries and visionaries. Jesus's famous temptation in the wilderness follows a similar pattern, although this is rarely noticed; his unusually high state of clarity following forty days of fasting and prayer allows him to quickly spot and disarm the trap set for him by the tempter: the subtle seductions of security ("Turn these stones into bread"), vainglory ("Throw yourself off this parapet and watch how the angels swoop down to rescue you!"), and power ("I will give you dominion over the entire world").[7] Even for the Son of Man, the capacity to read the signs of the times requires a responsible individual stewardship of one's lens of perception.

Whether such seeing is *inherently* an individual activity is, however, a matter of dispute. While the classic monastic archetype awards pride of place to the great solitaries (and that was the model that Rafe favored), both Gurdjieff and Teilhard were convinced, for different reasons, that the candlepower of consciousness is vastly strengthened in the synergy of a group. "Without a group, nothing is possible" was Gurdjieff's celebrated dictum, and his microhistory of Wisdom schools in *Beelzebub's Tales* offers abundant documentation of the principle at stake. Even if a revelation is initially received in solitude—as, for example, in the case of Ashiata Shiemash—it is quickly amplified and orchestrated in a school.

But equally often, it is the preexistence of the school that allows the revelation to be received in the first place. This was certainly the case with that primordial Wisdom school in Atlantis, and as Gurdjieff tells the tale, only through the comprehensive inner and outer preparation of its seven charter participants is the viewing screen set to a scale that will allow them to comprehend the magnitude of impending planetary catastrophe. The revelation is greater than an individual pixel of consciousness can hold, no matter how finely attuned. When we are working on a galactic scale, the heart that apprehends it is no longer the individual heart, but the *noetic heart of the imaginal body of humankind*, in which each fully prepared Wisdom group holographically participates.

While Gurdjieff and Teilhard most likely never crossed paths in actual physical life, I believe that Teilhard's remarkable "complexification/consciousness" theory may offer the real explanation for Gurdjieff's intuitively correct recognition of the group as the true instrument of higher spiritual discernment. From his long view as a paleontologist, Teilhard observed that over the entire 4.5-billion-year history of planetary evolution, each new leap in consciousness is accompanied by (and in fact depends on) a correlative leap in the complexity of the supporting physical structure (its "arrangement," as Teilhard calls it). Increasingly complex brains and nervous systems mark the journey from the simple earthworms and starfish to the staggering profundity of human thought and creativity. And it is under the conditions of constriction and convergence, forcing the entire system to fold in upon itself and begin to ramify internally, that this evolutionary complexification proceeds with the maximum efficiency.

If Teilhard's theory is correct, it is a fair surmise that the next levels of conscious emergence—into what is now popularly called "integral" and "nondual" consciousness—*will not happen simply through the domino-chain aggregation of individual enlightened psyches.* It will require the emergence of an accompanying new "physical arrangement," or *body* featuring an even greater degree of differentiated function within an overarching unity. Teilhard was already envisioning this new evolutionary body as the noosphere, and he had already grasped that its materiality was comprised not of corpuscular elements ordered by tangential energy, but of "thought" exchanged among humans through radial energy—or in other words, rephrased in the language of the Western Inner tradition, that *it would operate according to the substantiality and causality of World 24.* To the extent that the conscious circle bears witness to that higher imaginal body and in fact arises as a specific expression of it, I believe that groups and Wisdom schools are here to stay as the prime locus of conscious-circle activity as we approach that second axial threshold.

In favoring the group model over the time-hallowed solitary, however, one needs to be very careful not to fall back into outdated World 48 modalities. I still chuckle at my friend Ajahn Sona's priceless quip: "What's the plural of egoic? *We*-goic." Wegoic fellowship with all its tricky and laborious protocols is not the way this imaginal body orders itself, and Gurdjieff was very clear in expressing his disappointment when the Babylonian School fell back into such "wiseacreing." Mentally generated platforms and inflammatory rhetoric simply add to the pain body of this world. The first priority of a Wisdom school aspiring to conscious-circle partnership must be to maintain a consistently high level of imaginal clarity in which something new can actually be tasted. The synergy is itself the new vibration, the seeing is itself the doing, and all that's really needed is to hold that vibration for as long as one can, as purely as one can; then like water running downhill, it will find its way into the ground. "Truth has only to appear once, in one single mind," Teilhard averred shortly before his death, "for it to be impossible for anything to prevent it from spreading universally and setting everything ablaze."[8] How we get "from here to there" is the real measure of amplitude of the conscious circle when it is doing its job rightly.

Third Force

According to the Law of Three, all new arisings in whatever domain and at whatever scale are caused by the interweaving of *three* independent forces (not just two), which Gurdjieff calls affirming, denying, and reconciling. Where there are just two, there is impasse, and situations logjam. But since it is the nature of life in the created order, flowing as it does out of World 3, to be continuously moving and shapeshifting, third force enters. Impasses break up. New configurations emerge, for better or worse. This will either happen randomly, under the law of accident, or it will happen intentionally, under the law of fate. In the latter case it is an *imaginally generated* new arising, and the conscious circle often has a distinctive role to play.

Third force is a bit like quicksilver itself; under various lights it can appear to be generated, invoked, midwifed, or discovered in a situation—or it can emerge, seemingly out of left field, through a random event or "coincidence." The conscious circle can be deployed in any of these directions. While generally its role seems to be to maintain that deep reservoir of spacious, nonidentified attentiveness out of which third force most spontaneously arises, every so often it finds itself functioning directly as third force itself, providing that requisite bridging element that breaks up the logjam and ushers in the new configuration.

The history of civilization is marked by a few great turning points, when things which had apparently been moving in one direction suddenly shift course and move in another, often under mysterious circumstances. I do not want to fall into a magical retelling of history here, where every miraculous plot twist is taken as evidence of imaginal intervention. But as I ponder how third force has played out at some of these significant crossroads in human history, I would like to share three stories, all of them basically anecdotal, that appear to me to bear the particular fragrance of conscious-circle involvement.

The first story was told to me many years ago by my dear friend and teacher Murat Yagan, who trained extensively in the Abkhazian shamanic and Bektashi dervish lineages before emigrating to Canada in 1960 to take up work as a teacher of the deeper imaginal roots of the Western Inner tradition. According to Murat—and he was adamant about this—the origins of Sufism predate Islam and in fact lie in "the order of Melchizedek," or in other words, directly in the imaginal realm. The marriage of these two spiritualities was effected only in the ninth century through the deliberate intervention of a Central Asian Wisdom council, which directly foresaw that the external container of Islam would be the only vessel strong enough to withstand the devastation shortly to be unleashed by Mongol invasions. Moving quickly to protect a tender shoot of human consciousness beginning to bud in Central Asia, the council effected a union so sturdy that to this day the standard version of Islamic history claims that Sufism is simply "the mystical arm of Islam," generated entirely within an Islamic matrix.

Sometimes initial calamities, once viewed from the perspective of the conscious circle, begin to make sense in a whole different way. The Chinese invasion of Tibet in 1959 is just such an example and furnishes my second story. On the one hand, this violent act of aggression broke up a Wisdom enclave of almost supernatural purity and power. On the other hand, it displaced this Wisdom to the West, where it was sorely needed and well positioned to grow the entire world. As the Dalai Lama, Lama Yeshe, and others of that remarkable lineage made their way to Dharamshala and points west, the cross-pollination began in earnest, and the reinfusion of energy into the West's own contemplative traditions has laid a sturdy global foundation for the second axial awakening. Again, we see the deeper imaginal pattern at work: just as Israel's two great leaps of consciousness (from magical to "mythic membership" and from mythic membership to rational) were precipitated by a direct encounter with the Wisdom schools of Babylon and Egypt under circumstances initially presenting as calamitous, so our third collective planetary leap seems to bear evidence of a parallel Wisdom cross-pollination. And seeing that, one begins to relax, breathe again, and trust the pattern. If the long arc of history bends toward consciousness, the conscious circle will be bending the long arc.

"Is Paris Burning?"

My third story may be my own fantasy, but only the last connection; all the rest up to that point is verifiably true. During the dark days of World War II, when most spiritual teachers were fleeing for refuge to less war-torn places, Gurdjieff elected to stay put in Paris, in his tiny flat less than a quarter of a mile as the crow flies from the central command post of the German occupation. And in this bitter season of deprivation and hopelessness, he set about generating intentionally the energy of abundance, the missing element in a desperately traumatized world. Using skills he had gained who knows how, he managed to acquire huge stockpiles of food—not just basic staples always available in an unlocked pantry, but elegant luxuries, Armagnac and chocolates, served up in lavish banquets in an atmosphere suffused with the limitless possibility of the human spirit. Those who still remember those banquets know full well that the real food being served was love. A Babette's feast not of literary creation but carved in real-time flesh and blood.

Just over the hill, in the Place de la Concorde, during the summer of 1944, the noose was tightening on the Nazi occupation. The American troops had landed in Normandy and were steadily making their way toward Paris. An elaborate scheme had been set in place by those leading the German evacuation that would have left behind a swath of destruction obliterating some of the great monuments of human culture. Dietrich von Choltitz, a general widely known for his ruthlessness, was in charge of the operations. Explosives were placed under Notre Dame Cathedral and the Louvre. It is all detailed in the book *Is Paris Burning?*[9]

Somehow, it never happened. The reasons are still not clear. There was never a moment when it was decided *not* to blow up Paris. There were negotiations and communications right up to the end, but no moment of decision. Like the tide turning, the moment simply receded.

I could never prove that there was a connection between these two events. But knowing how imaginal causality works and Gurdjieff's skills in this realm, I cannot *not* believe it. In my heart I still fiercely hold it as his greatest gift to our West, and I offer up my prayers of gratitude. I will count him forever among the thirty-six.

Nine

SECOND BODY, ABLER SOUL

IN THE PREVIOUS chapter I pictured the conscious circle as a locus of intense exchange between advanced beings, some still living on this earth plane, others gone beyond it. This means, of course, that the exchange takes place within the domain of imaginal causality, and specifically through the vehicle of the second or kesdjan body, which is the common element between them. It is through the stabilization of this inner body that one is able to actively participate in the imaginal exchange.

In the Christian Inner tradition, this inner body is often referred to as "the wedding garment." The allusion here is to the apocalyptic parable in Matthew 22 in which, after the invited guests have all declined the invitation to the wedding banquet, the master of the banquet throws open the doors to the highways and byways. In an ironic final twist, however, only those guests who have had the foresight to bring their wedding garment can be admitted, and one late invitee finds himself summarily chucked out. This twist always defies and infuriates conventional scriptural exegesis, which sees the treatment as "unfair." But as in its twin apocalyptic parable of the ten bridesmaids (Matthew 25), the imaginal message is clear: unless one has already woven this garment in the alchemically transformed substance of one's life, the door cannot open. For it is specifically through the entrainment of these "wedding garments" (i.e., bodies of the same spiritualized materiality) that the communion between the realms is actually carried out.

For those of us still physically present on this earth plane, this inner body is "the life within our life," our nascent "Real I." It is the secret veiled by the form, the building slowly taking shape inside the scaffolding. From the imaginal perspective, however, it is our *actual body*, the true seat of our nontemporal selfhood. When we die, the scaffolding falls away and what has been created stands on its own. If our time of earthly existence has been spent in sincere inner striving, this kesdjan selfhood will already have quickened within the womb of our earthly life, and death presents no disruption to identity.[1]

This inner body has a far more fluid substantiality than our earthly notion of selfhood. But it still displays a distinct individual form and identity—a "tincture," as Jacob Boehme called it—clearly distinguishable from other tinctures. In the imaginal realm it is never a question of the drop dissolving into the ocean; this is still supremely the realm of the *personal*. But it is a lighter and far more intertwining personal, carried not so much in the drops themselves as in the current that flows between them. As Beatrice Bruteau once perceptively commented, "It may be that all true persons are circles whose centers are nowhere and whose circumferences are everywhere. And thus they may all overlap each other and interpenetrate each other with an intimacy we can scarcely imagine, because we think of intimacy and maintenance of individual personhood as inversely proportional."[2] This is a beautiful description of the paradoxical dance between particularity and fluidity that is quintessential to imaginal personhood, and certainly to the flow of exchange within the conscious circle of humanity.

At this level, rest assured that individual personhood does not yet drop out. Rather, finally shed of its egoic weight belt, it lives and vibrates with a life even more intensely its own.

If this notion stretches the imagination, it's actually one of the easiest inner teachings to verify in the outer religious tradition. We have a name for these highly attained beings in popular devotion. We call them "saints," and we pray to them. And we don't mix them up. Mary Magdalene is never mistaken for Mother Mary; St. Francis, St. Peter, St. Joseph all come to us as distinctively real fragrances, absolutely continuous with the inner energy they bore while still in bodily life. They are as distinctive as flowers in a garden. And so it is with imaginal selfhood: personal identity is carried in a much more subtle and diaphanous form, yet it is clearly distinguishable as personal identity. I know Rafe as distinctly when he shows up on my inner screen as I did back in those days when he rolled into my driveway, brakes squealing, in his old Scout. And it is exactly the same Rafe presence that he announces.

Building Second Body

The quickening of this kesdjan body thus comprises both the precondition and the vehicle for participation in the conscious circle on both sides of the divide, and jump-starting that process in me was the work that Rafe set himself to in earnest during our human time together, under no illusion that we would be more than barely underway by the time his own physical death rolled around. He tended to look upon the entire Gurdjieff Work as a heroic attempt to reestablish the conditions in which our earthly life does in fact become the birthing ground for this finer and more cosmically durable "other," needed not for personal glory but for cosmic service.

We have already spent some time in earlier chapters

looking at the specific practices through which second body is built, so I will revisit them only briefly here. The twin pillars of Gurdjieff's transformational program are of course conscious labor and intentional suffering, and a faithful self-exertion on these two treadmills during the time of this life will in most cases bring about a steady growth in the radiance and stability of second-body presence. Undergirding both of these pillars, however, is the deeper intention to move *off* the attraction/aversion treadmill, which chains selfhood to the physical body and the ephemeral selfhood of this world. Second body essentially emerges as the fruit of that liberation. As Maurice Nicoll described it in a passage particularly well loved by Rafe: "The man who has reached a stage in which he has something independent of failure and success, cold or heat, comfort or discomfort, starvation or plenty, such a man has second body."[3] Expanding on this same insight, Valentin Tomberg further describes the second body as "an etheric body independent of life forces that can draw its energy directly from the Spiritual life world."[4]

You may recall that in chapter 3 I mentioned in passing that second body emerges as the alchemical byproduct of the "upward transmission of energies through the intermediary of conscious attention." I was alluding here to what I have now specifically termed "cosmic dialysis," and since this comprises so much of the ongoing work of the conscious circle, it may be worth rereading that paragraph in full (see page 60) before continuing.

Force

I want to make very clear that conscious exchange between the realms is no metaphor. It is not simply a matter of lifting up one's hands into thin air and receiving a fairy-tale blessing.

There is an actual energetic exchange between the realms, and the medium of exchange is in fact a very fine and high vibrational quality of attention, which appears to us in this realm as a form of psychic (or radial) energy, but in the imaginal realm is an actual *substance*, kinetic and highly potent. You might picture it as the "bloodstream" of the kesdjan body (Gurdjieff called it "hanbledzoin"), and clearing a channel for this high-energy substance to flow through one's still-human frame without causing internal or external damage requires a rigorous inner preparation and a continuing outer vigilance.

"Conscious attention is an instrument that vibrates like a crystal at its own frequency," writes William Segal in "The Force of Attention," the essay to which I have already referred many times. "Cleared of all internal noise . . . it is free to receive the signals broadcast at each moment from a creative universe in communication with all creatures." That is the heart of the energetic exchange within the conscious circle, and it is important to remember who these players from the other side are. They are the *attained ones*, the ones who during the time of this life have managed to crystallize something within themselves that allows a powerful personal continuance beyond physical death. Such people are of a higher order of substantiality, and the force that flows through this exchange is not to be underestimated. "A man without a body is infinitely more alive than a man with a body," my dervish teacher Murat Yagan always insisted—at least for those who have crossed this critical kesdjan threshold. In 2015, when I visited the tombs of some of the Naqshbandi Sufi saints who were among Murat's spiritual forebears, I could see exactly what he meant. The blast of spiritual energy emerging from those tombs literally knocked me off my feet. These conscious beings on the other side do indeed emit force; that is the mode of transmission. It is felt typically not so much as a vision or a message (both too slow), but as an *instantaneous knowing* conveyed in the characteristic energetic signature of that being. Force is conveyed, and force is received.

In classical hagiography this force is often depicted as a nimbus, a halo of light surrounding a saint's head. We would do well to pay close attention to the energetics actually being portrayed in this traditional symbolism. "Light shines out from the center of a being of light and illuminates the whole cosmos," says the Gospel of Thomas in logion 24. As second body grows inside a living human being, the candlepower and directional force of this light increases substantially, sometimes geometrically. The B-influence teacher metamorphizes into a C-influence teacher, capable of conveying baraka, an energetic transmission that temporarily elevates the state of its recipient. There is a current flowing through one's physical body that can be sensed both directly and by others. It is a sign that the energy drawn directly from "the spiritual life world" has indeed become one's sustaining food, and the transition to kesdjan selfhood is well underway.

This growing gift confers a growing responsibility; we have spoken about this already as well. To parade it as a sign of one's spiritual attainment is a gross and dangerous miscalculation. The gift must not be hidden, but it must sometimes be veiled so as not to harm those not yet prepared to receive it. And it must never be forgotten that wielding even this relatively modest amount of authentic spiritual power brings with it some solemn accountabilities. As the contemporary spiritual master Hameed Ali wisely counseled my friend Russ Hudson, "You must take responsibility for what has been cultivated in you." Sometimes this responsibility does, indeed, require closing the doors on what once looked like open options in your life, as you come to recognize that the seed that quickened within you now holds a lien on your life.

Temporary Permanent Individuality

The Inner tradition is unanimous in its insistence that the work of quickening second body must be begun in *this* realm, while still in the conditions of earthly life. It is the strength, intensity, and courage of the soul's "pure becoming" in *this* world that determines its agency in the next. After the cessation of earthly temporality, "there will be no bettering, but everything remaineth as it returneth home," according to Jacob Boehme.[5] No further growth is possible.

Personally, I have always rested a bit uneasily with the second part of that instruction. It seems a bit too much like the superimposition of a lower-order causality (where growth is understood to be a function of time) upon a higher order one, as well as a rather arbitrary curtailment of the freedom of higher realms to do exactly as they please. Gurdjieff, one of the dissenting voices here, argues emphatically in *Beelzebub's Tales* that, once a certain critical threshold of crystallization has been attained here below, the journey of soul-making goes on uninterrupted (no friction of time to slow it down!) until arriving at its ultimate endpoint in the full attainment of a "permanent individuality" viable in all cosmoses of the created order. Along the entire Ray of Creation, at whatever point we find ourselves, help and blessing (and yes, the occasional miracle) flow to us freely from a greater cosmic benevolence solidly in our camp.

But as a practical starting point, it is no doubt wise to heed the consensus that it is useful and highly recommended to begin the work of building second body here and now, while still under the protective coloration of earthly form. The conditions for this inner development are particularly congenial here (in fact, that is the only way one can really make sense of the otherwise staggeringly difficult outer conditions of earthly life), and through the mediation of the conscious circle, our work goes on in two worlds at once, and our cosmos is doubly blessed.

The kesdjan body represents the lowest rung on a ladder of increasingly fine gradations of "Real I," or permanent individuality. It is what "gets you through the gate," so to speak, into the wedding banquet, but it is still a long way off from the permanent individuality that we humans are so quick to arrogate to our "souls," even those souls completely ungerminated and untransformed in this life. Kesdjan selfhood possesses what you might think of as "temporary permanent individuality"; it is immortal within the sphere of the personal (Worlds 12, 24, and 48), and it is the instrument par excellence for participation in the operations of the imaginal ream. But it is a *transitional* body in every respect, and its term limits are set as one nears the far end of World 12. Beyond that, as one moves beyond the sphere of the personal and into the causal, a different body is needed, of yet more crystalline substantiality, that will carry one beyond the realm of the personal.

The "duration" of one's sojourn in the still-mutable selfhood of the subtle realms is also, in some sense, a repeat of the scenario I have just described, though at the next level up: just as our earthly realm affords the "protective coloration" for the growth of second body, so the imaginal and Christic realms provide the normal protective coloration for the growth of the third and fourth, the astral and the causal, respectively. The "duration" of one's sojourn in the personal realms is to some degree determined by the length of gestation required by these more subtle bodies, and throughout this gestation help is again received—not only from the higher realms, but remarkably, from the lower as well. I will return to this point shortly.

In any case, it must again be emphasized that the kesdjan

body does not yet possess full permanent individuality. There will be a second death, a "second rascooarno" as Gurdjieff forewarned, that marks the dissolution of our personal self-hood and the "birth" into a causality that will either appear to us as total dissolution, or life at such an intense vibrational fineness that it does not even register on the normal screen of human consciousness.

This realization calls forth a final and as yet unmentioned aspect of the work that goes on from our human end of the conscious circle of humanity: support for the continued spiritual growth of those on the other side. These advanced beings are themselves in a state of growth and transition, well along on the next leg of their journey toward permanent individuality. As we join them in the conscious circle, the partnership furnishes the opportunity for them to grow still further in what Boehme calls "majesty" and "mobility"—the *incandescence* of their presence and the *scope* of their agency. Toward this end we are able to offer our support, sometimes simply by providing the occasion for the continued growth and testing of their spiritual wingspan; at other times in the form of further purification and healing for those shadow elements as yet unreconciled within them (and no, these do not simply fall away with the provisional self; the deeper wounds await deeper healing in the imaginal and Christic bandwidths before final liberation from the personal realms is possible).

Gurdjieff was quick to recognize the extraordinarily hopeful message embedded in the traditional concept of purgatory, so distasteful to our modern sensibilities: that prayers and blessings from the living can and do reach our beloved ones no longer in physical life and continue their work of healing and transformation. He even named the most sacred planet in his mythic galaxy "Holy Planet Purgatory," where advanced souls would eventually need to make their way to await their final transfiguration. His insight here brings with it the powerful reminder that reciprocal feeding is indeed reciprocal. Just as a tiny twig thrown into a woodstove can set a smoldering log burning again, so the smallest twigs of our human faithfulness and love can rekindle the heart of even a sorrowing great one.

The Abler Soul

In most cases, the vehicle for participation in the conscious circle is one's individual kesdjan body. That is what those earlier parables we noted (the wedding garment and the lamp oil of the ten bridesmaids) were proclaiming. One's kesdjan body is individually quickened through the quality and quantity of one's own individual striving. It is normally nontransferable.

But there are exceptions to this rule.

The abler soul represents a special case within the overall pattern of conscious-circle partnership in which the bridge between the realms is specifically localized in the single kesdjan body shared by two beloveds who find themselves temporarily stranded on either side of the vale of death. While still in the time of this life the beloveds (who are obviously not strangers to the spiritual path) covenant to fuse a joint kesdjan body which will serve as the vehicle both for a particularly intimate and efficacious kind of transmission between the realms and also for the continued growth of each one of them in the direction of true permanent individuality.

While authentic bonds between the realms can be formed between any kind of human beloveds—parent and child, brother and sister, teacher and student—the "abler soul" bond is unique because it works directly with the fire of transfigured eros (the sexual energy), to accomplish the work of fusion. This World 6 energy is seen by many esoteric teachers (most notably J. G. Bennett) as being the finest substance humans can work with while still in physical flesh, and it is in any case what gives this particular configuration its extraordinary generative potency.

It was Boris Mouravieff, a maverick Gurdjieffian with strong Orthodox proclivities, who first fully articulated this possibility in his three-volume study *Gnosis*.[6] Mouravieff named this path of transformation the "Fifth Way," a deliberate play on Gurdjieff's celebrated Fourth Way. If the Fourth Way is the path of conscious man, who through painstaking inner work gradually crystallizes second body within himself, the Fifth Way is this same path of conscious labor and intentional suffering willingly undertaken in intimate partnership with a human beloved. It is the path of conscious love. It burns away the psychological dross with lightning rapidity, both in its mirroring capacity and in the profound transfiguration of the heart in its total immolation on the altar of the beloved. "True love requires sacrifice," wrote another anonymous postulant on this path, "because true love is a transforming force and is itself the birth pangs of union on a higher level."[7] That is indeed the essence of this fiery, all-consuming path.

From the perspective of the worlds, this Fifth Way path also shows forth in an extremely concentrated way what love looks like right at the eye of the needle, where the $a = ek$ transfiguration is going on in full force. Hence, it releases into the world a very strong infusion of pure agape and a direct connection to World 12, where divine eros, fully apprivoisé in its journey through the finite realms, is handed back into the infinite in that innermost sanctum of that "hidden treasure longing to be known."

When Rafe died, I suddenly inherited an abler soul. We'd been working in that direction anyway, but it was delivered the night of his requiem vigil with a rapidity and force that left us both slightly startled. From my end, certainly, it took a while to get used to this new state of affairs. I remember one afternoon a few months into the grieving, I was doing the full-on Mary Magdalene dumb blonde in the Garden of Gethsemane routine—"But gardener, please, I want to see his *body!*"—when Rafe suddenly cut across the whole pathetic drama with a single karate-chop snort: "Your *life* is my body." I got it. In this hobbledehoy three-legged race we now found ourselves in, every decision I made, every impression I took in, every road taken or not taken, would be the outer form of our inner union. For better or worse we would grow this body together.

Certainly over these two decades there has been more than a little satisfaction watching us both grow. There was always an authentic Shams-and-Rumi configuration to our relationship, where it was implicitly understood that I would take Rafe's brilliant intuitive seeing and translate it into a teaching. As appreciation of his spiritual giftedness has steadily grown through this exposure, it has been gratifying to note the parallel increase in his own majesty and mobility as he strides across the imaginal and Christic realms toward the place where I suspect his spiritual destiny has lain all along, the causal. As I mentioned at the beginning, it was not by accident that some intuitive abbot gave him the monastic name "Raphael"; the archangelic scepter was already obscurely visible, even beneath his old work jeans and cowboy boots.

As for me, it has been a wild ride. My own spiritual emergence has been effortlessly supported as I work and teach out of our combined spiritual knowledge, transparently available to me through our kesdjan common ground. The unnerving aspect of this, of course, is that I know more than I know, and I often find myself teaching from beyond my own level of spiritual attainment individually integrated and grounded. It's not about channeling Rafe, nor is it simply lip-synching what he taught me; we are definitely both breaking new ground together. But I am always uneasily aware that there is a gap between what I know and can sustain in union with him and what I know and can sustain in my own right. It was exactly this gap that so infuriated Johnny, spiritual intuitive that he is; he could only see it as hypocrisy. Whether it's that or just Peter walking on the water I'm still not sure, but I do know that I share his uneasiness on this point, and that it probably factored way more than I suspected in what would eventually fall out of our winter odyssey.

So what about this abler soul when I, too, am on the other side? Already I am older now than Rafe was when he left this planet, and as his own cosmic wingspan continues to spread, it is clear that he has at this point all but outgrown this kesdjan vehicle. What then of our "temporary permanent individuality?" Does it give way in the direction of permanent individuality or permanent dissolution? Will I slipstream my way straight into the second rascooarno, or am I headed toward Cinderella at midnight, about to watch my wedding garment turn back into rags?

"Hush," says Rafe. "You'll see. Nothing is taken away."

Above Ground and Flowing Hard

It's always a mistake to draw the timeline too tightly around one's own era. From our limited historical perspective, every era feels to itself like the eye of the imaginal needle, and the current buzz emerging from New Age circles that our own era is on the leading edge of an imminent second-axial breakthrough must be taken with more than a grain of Teilhardian salt, remembering that for Teilhard the rising tide of consciousness is measured in geological eons, not human decades.

And yet, that being said, there do seem to be some features

of the moment we now find ourselves in that invite us to pay attention in a special way. I have mentioned already how Wisdom schools tend to come above ground either on the cusps of great forward leaps in consciousness or in times of planetary destabilization, and we have seen how our own era qualifies on both counts. To these markers I would now add a third, the one which has really put me on full alert as to likely imaginal intervention. Within my own immediate Christian lineage it seems that there has been a marked and accelerating exodus of spiritual masters to the other side. Joining Rafe, who departed in 1995, are now Raimon Panikkar (2010), Murat Yagan (2013), Beatrice Bruteau (2014), Bruno Barnhart (2015), Bernadette Roberts (2017), and in October 2018, Thomas Keating and Joseph Boyle, whose highly configured "double helix" passing I will reflect on in my concluding trope. Nearly all the people who were once my personal teachers and whose wisdom shines forth brightly from these pages are now on the other side.

While this is in some sense the inevitable course of things when one finds herself in her seventies, both the rate and the configuration seem a little too pointed to ignore. In imaginal causality the reason is not hard to spot: their force is greatly enhanced there. As long as there are willing hands to join them from this side, the work goes on far more powerfully in this new configuration, particularly where that work involves plunging to "the heart of the earth" both ecologically, to the place from which Jesus embraced and sanctified the constructal givens of this realm, and metaphorically, into the deep structures of the Christian theological imagination, which will need to be systematically reframed on a nondual basis if Christianity is to remain a serious player in the next stage of our collective conscious evolution. And so this displacement toward the more imaginally embodied side of the conscious circle strikes me fundamentally as a great sign of hope. Important and powerful shifts are indeed about to befall our *mixtus orbis* and are in fact already underway. Here on our flesh-and-blood end of the stick, the time for daydreaming and demurring is over. All hands are needed on deck.

Trope

THOMAS AND JOSEPH

THOMAS KEATING IS of course widely known. As the chief
architect of Centering Prayer and one of the patriarchs of the
Christian contemplative reawakening, he bore real force in
this world. I am privileged to have known him as my teacher
and spiritual father for more than thirty years and to witness
his own steady growth, particularly in the last five years of his
life, toward a truly global and nondual consciousness. He
lived a long, long life, till the age of ninety-five, and for most
of those last five years, our annual visits would begin with his
solemn announcement, "This will be the last time you will see
me in human life." It did not wind up that way, however; somehow it was given to me to be in his presence three more times
as he came down the home stretch, then seated right next to
his body during his overpoweringly intense requiem mass at
the Trappist motherhouse in Spencer, Massachusetts—truly
a cosmic initiation. It was a wonder and a privilege to watch a
brilliant life of seeking and service come full term.

Joseph Boyle is a more intimately shared treasure. He wrote
no books, gave very few public events (and those only under
duress), and preferred the more hidden life of the traditional
monastic pathway. Sixty of the seventy-seven years of his life
were lived as a monk, the last thirty of them as the well-loved
abbot of St. Benedict's Monastery in Snowmass. He entered
the community at the age of eighteen, and Thomas Keating was his abbot. Later the terms reversed, and he became

Thomas's abbot; they played abbatial leapfrog for sixty years. Joseph was the one who gave Thomas permission to color outside the lines of Trappist institutional life, and he in fact put the entire monastery at the service of Thomas's bold vision of a "contemplative outreach." He was also, incidentally, the abbot who gave his blessing for Rafe and me to continue our admittedly pushing-the-envelope relationship. "I saw it was helping him," said Joseph. For Joseph, the role of abbot as spiritual father was absolutely first priority; everything in him bent toward helping each man grow in exactly the way that would bring him to fullness in his own unique self-expression of Christic love. Whatever it took.

Joseph did not consider himself an intellectual man. He beat up on himself for not spending more time reading, but in truth, he endured even those obligatory reading duties as time spent away from what he really loved: reading the heartbeat of the world around him. He would rather hike in the mountains, gaze at the night skies, and personally welcome the steady stream of visitors who, attracted by the hospitality that naturally radiated from him, would return again and again for worship and retreats. Together, over the years, Joseph and all those people cocreated "the magic monastery" (as Theophane, one of the brethren, dubbed it), a tiny monastic Camelot of human thriving and joy.

In the last decade of their lives, I could witness the gradual transfiguration of both men. Still very much their own human selves, Thomas became increasingly the embodiment of what Gurdjieff would call "higher intellectual center." His clarity grew in leaps and bounds, along with the force of his presence and the scope of his universal vision. Joseph became more and more the embodiment of pure heart, higher emotional center. At some point it occurred to me with a start that they were now a World 12 and World 6 tag team. Joseph was melting rapidly into a pure radiance of love, like a glowing coal that can give off nothing but warmth. Thomas was becoming immortal diamond. Fiercely clear, filled with love, but love of a more adamantine, transpersonal quality, less in dialogue with the emotions of this world and more in dialogue with "the sorrow of our Common Father," as is surely befitting when the gift of transformed agape is handed back into the causal realms in a fontal upwelling of cosmic mercy.

And as they had lived together, so it appeared that they were destined to die together, their human lives mysteriously interwoven on that imaginal loom. In early January 2018, as I was plying the Caribbean aboard *Zoi*, a phone call arrived that Thomas had been hospitalized for yet another serious bronchial infection and that Joseph had been diagnosed with a cancer pressing on his gallbladder. The winter passed. Thomas recovered but steadily lost strength in his lower body and by spring was essentially nonambulatory. Joseph did a brutal round of surgery followed by chemo and radiation and returned to St. Benedict's Monastery to convalesce. In April the decision was made to transfer Thomas back to the motherhouse in Spencer where he could receive full-time infirmary care. Joseph's cancer backed off briefly, but by the end of the summer it had aggressively returned. By early fall both men lay dying.

Thus began the extraordinary final chapter.

Joseph's death came first, by four days, on October 21, 2018. He left as he had lived, gracefully surrendered, laughing and comforting his friends, eyes fixed gently on Christ. It was as noiseless as the snow melting in spring.

Thomas's death was, I think it can be said without exaggeration, unexpectedly difficult. To everyone's consternation, not the least his own, he lived for nearly a month beyond what the infirmarian had given as the outside limit that his body would survive, sustained in total on three boiled eggs and a daily few sips of water. Two weeks before his death he sat bolt upright in bed and delivered a powerful seven-minute oracle, speaking to the entire world from a place well beyond this world in a stern injunction to lay down arms and take up the path of universal trust and compassion. I have listened to that message, hastily recorded on a monk's cell phone, and it rivets the soul. He spoke from a place of total cosmic nakedness—"no place to go, no proof of anything, no fundamental face," as he described it. He was done with constructal zones, even those most deeply cherished. I could feel him flying by the seat of his pants in a kind of "out the gate" cosmic freefall. And yet right up to the end, there was also shadow material to face, anguish of soul and anguish of body as well. It was a profound scourging, a dredging of the channel to a depth that no one would have thought such a saintly man deserved or would endure. "Sometimes people seem to get the wrong death," as the young novice Constance observes in Poulenc's *Dialogue of the Carmelites*.

But no, it was not the wrong death, for immediately after his final painful breath the transfiguration began in earnest. The entire room immediately filled with fragrance (this is by testimony of the two monks who were present with him that night), and his face relaxed into deep sweetness. Even after having lain on his back for nearly a month, his body was found to be entirely free of bedsores—indeed when I stood beside him at his funeral a week later, I had the overwhelming impression that his body had not shriveled or wizened; it had merely *vanished*. He was a slightly scale-model version of himself, but he was completely intact, powerful, and majestically craggy as he presided over the space of his requiem mass with the force of a Moses perched on his mountain crag. His was a "rainbow body" type of death, well known in Tibetan Buddhist tradition but not usually seen in the Christian circles, where spiritual attainment beyond the Christic realms is not really encouraged. Thomas went straight through two realms at once, dying not only the first but also the second rascooarno in those anguished weeks in Spencer. It was a cataclysmic transition and leaves me with little doubt that his service in the conscious circle is now wielded from the causal level.

But he could not have done it without Joseph. Of that I am certain. The spiritual "rightness" of their intertwined lives and deaths was intuitively grasped by nearly everyone, and I myself spoke of it metaphorically in an intercession I offered at Snowmass the morning Thomas's death was announced: "May the double helix of their lives be the DNA and RNA of a new genetic code of love." Without some common knowledge of the underlying esoteric ground, it was hard to be much more precise than that. But since we have now spent an entire book laying that groundwork, I would like to offer here my best take on what actually seems to me to been going on, particularly as it bears on the work of the conscious circle of humanity.

According to the Law of Three, you recall, "the higher blends with the lower in order to activate the middle." Between World 6 and World 24 lies World 12, the Christic; and if Thomas now exercises causal agency, World 12 becomes the new middle between his sphere of influence and our ability to receive it as imaginal sustenance. In his beautiful instantiation of that Christic presence, Joseph offers himself as the bridge. His gentle, joyful personhood, now fully incorporated into the mystical body of Christ, allows Thomas's causal force to be received and filtered gracefully into imaginal modalities. At the same time it sets Thomas free on the higher plane, no longer needing to veil the Shekinah shining so powerfully from his being, but now fully at liberty to wield it directly as a transforming and causally regenerative force.

They essentially present themselves now as a living icon of what mystical theology calls "the two natures of Christ"—logoic and human, fused in a single stream of love. They also furnish a powerful icon of conscious-circle exchange bumped up a notch—now in the 6-12-24 configuration realms rather than the 12-24-48 we have been considering so far. This is very good news for our planet and very good news for Christianity as well, auguring a powerful reawakening of its true mystical and cosmological epicenter. And so despite the disruption, I take heart; a bright new constellation has arisen in the morning skies.

Ten

THE SECOND RASCOOARNO

This is how I would die:
Into the Love I have for you
As pieces of cloud dissolve in sunlight

—RUMI

FOR MOST OF the past two decades I have lived with the expectation firmly before me that at the end of this three-legged race across two realms, there would be a reunion. Rafe and I would meet again face-to-face in a moment of pure ecstasy, at which point this kesdjan vehicle which held us together for so long would finally melt away to reveal the permanent form of our union of hearts. The second rascooarno, solemnized in our abler soul.

And that may still be the case. If it is, I will surely receive it with joy.

But if truth be told, I find myself starting to set less and less store by it. It's not that my mind has changed, in the sense that I think my calculations were in error. Quite to the contrary. It's still my best take based on the maps I've been steering by all these years and which I've shared with you in these pages. A construction the whole thing may be, but if so, it has proved itself over the years to have been a particularly sturdy and fruitful one, conferring both insight and blessing. It has served me well.

But my mind *has* changed in another way, in the sense that it's now no longer quite the same mind poring over all these maps, trying to make sense out of all these complexities. There are two ways that a map can come to the end of its useful life. The first is when it carries you all the way to your destination, and it's no longer needed because you've arrived. The second is when something shifts so deeply inside you that any need or desire for a map simply disappears. I've noticed this shift in me even over the several months I've been actively working on this book. It's not that I don't think about these "last things" anymore; I just don't think about them so much, or so much in that same way. These days I'm finding myself less and less interested in discovering what lies at the end of the rainbow and more and more interested in discovering what lies at the end of this hall of mirrors I call my mind.

This shift I attribute in large part to the tricksy spirit who sailed into my heart two winters ago and shoved it right into the eye of the needle.

 do

"Although some illusions are constructions, not all constructions are illusions." In her book *Old Age*, Helen Luke takes up this koan full bore in her searing exegesis of Shakespeare's *The Tempest*, the heart and soul of her iconic final work. Her eyes are riveted, with good reason, on the powerful and mysterious moment when Prospero, the great wizard, having accomplished all the tasks that his life would seem to require of him, decides in a sudden conversion of heart to release Ariel, the magical spirit-being who has served him all these years and brought him to the height of his powers. Good Jungian that she is, Luke senses the numinous force here. "What does it mean for a man or woman approaching death to set free the Ariel in himself—to break the staff and drown the book?" she asks.[1] Then, she immediately answers her own question in a single arresting comment: "In order to find an answer an individual must seek in the unconscious for his or her own image of an Ariel—that 'tricksy spirit'—and recreate him in imagination until his reality in the psyche is recognized."

The moment of release is a line gale parting the seasons of Prospero's life. On the one side he wears a wizard's robe and magically bends people and elemental forces to his will. On the other side, he stands before the audience stripped and naked, openly confessing his own vulnerability and need of prayer:

Now I want
spirits to enforce, art to enchant;
and my ending is despair unless it be relieved by prayer.
Which pierces so that it assaults
Mercy itself and frees all faults.[2]

What does it mean to let go of all that has carried one in one's life? What lies on the other side of such a vast and reckless self-donation?

It sounds to me a little bit like the second rascooarno.

Yes, I know that technically, the second rascooarno is the breakdown of the kesdjan body that ushers the way into the next level of subtle manifestation. But metaphorically, this means a deeper dying, a dying to all you know and to all that has brought you to where you are now. And in that sense, the second rascooarno is no stranger; we rehearse it in every passage of our life courageously embraced and then willingly let go. In linear time it may be "second," but in imaginal time it is primary; it furnishes the fundamental pattern.

 re

The icon of Prospero was already fermenting in my mind last spring when I wrote "Prospero, Jonah, and The Greek," my first run-up on these questions. Imaginal synchronicity being what it is, it came as no real surprise that between the time I began work on this book and the time I completed it, a live production of *The Tempest* providentially fell into my lap, courtesy of our local summer theater troupe, a group of highly creative younger artists, mostly out of New York City. Not only did they decide to stage the play in open air, on a secluded point of land jutting out into Deer Isle Thorofare, they also cast a woman in the role of Prospero. I wouldn't have thought it possible, but she carried it off powerfully and with a style and physical demeanor uncannily similar to my own. I watched spellbound for two hours as my life flashed before my eyes. I even persuaded the Greek to come, and we would have brought it off, were it not for the fact that Jonah & Co. had one more round of dirty tricks up their sleeves. I'll tell you that story in a little while.

Part of what makes *The Tempest* so compelling as a metaphysical inquiry is that Prospero's magical constructions cannot simply be dismissed as illusions. Over the years they have accomplished much good. Through his intricate spells and wizardry—and no less through his fierce óptimism and the demiurgic force he has bound to himself through Ariel— he has re-righted himself after unspeakable human treachery, brought his daughter safely through the storms, and ultimately restored her to wholeness and human community through his last great ruse, which traps her future husband on their enchanted island. As the play ends, all are restored to their right minds, set free to be themselves. The scoundrels are forgiven, the captives are released; the social order is returned to harmony. The construction has served its function; it can be laid down not because it has failed, but because it has succeeded brilliantly.

Of course, you know I feel much the same way about the imaginal realm. A construction it may be, but it is definitely a construction through which much good is accomplished, where the demiurgic force of creation itself—call it "the love that moves the sun and the stars"—is placed in service of this all-too-finite *mixtus orbis*. I have spent so much time in these pages intricately laying out its metaphysics, cosmology, causality, and protocols (and hopefully, evoking some sense of its beauty as well) because I sincerely believe it offers the very best map available for the reengagement of our visionary imagination and our intrinsic human generosity. It is a map large enough to contain our collective hearts and to point our species toward a greater sense of accountability, nobility, and God knows, *vastness*; to the real scale of the thing. If we are to be here on this planet at all, we might as well be here wisely and kindly, joyfully and creatively, making of "this fragile earth, our island home" (in the words of the Episcopal Book of Common Prayer), a place of healing and wonder, not boredom and mean-spiritedness. To the extent that this imaginal construction delivers all of the above, it has earned its place.

And frankly, I love the magic that goes on here. I cannot imagine a better cosmic home to have dwelled in all these years, artist and seeker sides of myself both fully engaged. It is a place where one may drink freely from those demiurgic springs that flood the soul with hope. And if I have indeed called upon my wizard's staff and book yet one more time to weave this imaginal castle before your eyes, it is because I know that whatever it is that wants to be spoken from that place into our world is important and very needed right now. The one thing for certain when I returned from my winter odyssey is that I had to *write,* and that is what I have done.

But living on this rapturous edge is also living on borrowed time, as Prospero himself already mysteriously knows, for the power being wielded here is not yet truly his own, but Ariel's. "He who binds unto himself a joy / doth the winged life destroy," Helen Luke comments, appropriately invoking William Blake. She makes curiously little, however, of the fact that this is actually a double bind, for the same force of will that holds Ariel captive equally traps Prospero in the enchanted circle of his own imagination. Where demiurgic power serves the personal will, there is as yet no real inner truth; there is only enchantment. And so the moment will arrive—*must* arrive—built into the terms from the beginning, when Ariel will once again press for his freedom. And miraculously, this time the heart will crack wide open, and what is asked will be given. Then and only then will the true healing begin.

mi

The Greek agreed, grudgingly, to go to the play. We struck a deal. We would go by sea, in his inflatable skiff. The waters are open to all and supremely his comfort zone so we figured it would be manageable. On the day of the Saturday matinee we took off from the town wharf, gunkholed our way into the small cove behind the main stage area, and found ourselves a fine watery viewing spot. So far so good. Johnny, jaunty and gregarious as ever, maneuvered in close to the beach and tried to engage Caliban, who was taking up his hiding place on the edge of the bank, from which he would shortly make his grand appearance. Caliban was not amused. He disappeared briefly and evidently had words with the production crew, for shortly afterward the theater manager showed up and moved us on, mumbling vaguely about "the safety of the actors." Stung by the rebuff, the Greek pulled on the starter cord with a particularly voracious yank, clearly intent to leave a wake behind that itself would "break the staff and drown the book." It was just then that our Jonah electromagnetic bad karma decided to kick in once again, and the little outboard that had never failed refused stubbornly through twenty pulls to start. So there we sat, a hilarious unintended prep band, Johnny pulling and cursing, me paddling frantically with the little spare paddle, disgracing ourselves publicly for one and all to see. So much for our grand Shakespeare adventure. Maybe in the next incarnation.

And well, for all the ruefulness of it, the black humor was also just too delicious. You could almost hear the old joke revving up: "Once upon a time there were three men in a boat: Prospero, Jonah, and the Greek. . ." Who was this imaginal trickster, anyway, who kept scrambling our path? We eventually got the motor going and retreated to a small island on the opposite side of the harbor to lick our wounds, sprawl out together on a rock, and laugh ourselves senseless. It was a brief halcyon moment in that brief halcyon summer, before our hourglass of grace finally ran out.

 fa

For Prospero, that hourglass moment arrives by surprise. The certainty of its arrival has never been in question, but the timing catches everyone a little off guard. It could just as easily have been tomorrow, or the day after tomorrow, or a thousand more tomorrows. But it is now.

It begins innocently enough, almost out of left field, in the afterglow of Prospero's greatest coup. Again, Ariel gently presses for his freedom. But Prospero, still savoring the sweetness of his triumph, first wants the full reportage. How diabolically brilliant was his son et lumière? How much did he make them all suffer? And Ariel can only report that they all seemed sad, the old lord Gonzalo with tears running down his beard. Then he adds his zinger, which of course Helen Luke bores right in on: "If you now beheld them, your affections would have become tender."

Prospero: Dost thou think so, spirit?
Ariel: Mine would, Sir, were I human.
Prospero: And mine shall.
Hast thou, which art but air, a touch, a feeling
Of their afflictions? And shall not myself,
One of their kind, that relish all as sharply
Passion as they, be kindlier moved than thou art?[3]

What Prospero could never allow himself to see while still intoxicated by his own magical powers is accomplished instantly in a moment of authentic remorse of conscience. How could this barely embodied spirit feel something that he in his own full humanity could not? Stung to the quick, he looks upon former antagonists and for the first time feels their distress. He looks upon this strange creature standing before him and feels compassion for him as well. This elusive spirit-being has tried his very best to be a good servant, but it is not in his nature; his nature is to be free. The moment rises up in Prospero like a geyser. "My charms I'll break, their senses I'll restore. . . . This rough magic I here abjure."

He has done it, finally; he has seen the world from beyond the "magnetical hunger"[4] of his own will, and the seeing is shattering. In our Stonington production, the intrinsic pathos was dramatically reinforced: Ariel immediately broke into a weird, unearthly vocalization and without a backward glance bounded down the hill and disappeared toward the sea. Immediately into my mind came that haunting final image in e. e. cummings's poignant love sonnet:

If this should be, I say if this should be
You of my heart, send me a little word;
That I may go to him, and take his hands,
Saying, Accept all happiness from me.
Then shall I turn my face, and hear one bird
Sing terribly afar in the lost lands.[5]

Prospero waits on the bank, absolutely still, until Ariel's madcap song is no longer heard. The old wizard is now doubly stripped—not only of the magic of his powers but of the magical power of intimacy. Gone now from his life will be both his daughter, who for all these years was his sole human grounding, and this wild, fontal companion from whom he drew the strength to live and the boldness to imagine. The hiding places also are gone; he can no longer use his book, the enormous creative power of his intellect, or his staff, the magical power of his will, to rescue himself from the now-inevitable encounter with what lies beyond the hall of mirrors of his mind. He is about to die the second rascooarno.

 sol

I paddled back out to that same small island a few weeks later, on the day when it all finally ended with the Greek. With one final murderous glare hurled in my direction, Johnny blazed his way out of Stonington harbor, his face set like flint toward the open sea. I found my way back to the rock where we'd laughed so hard together, and then with clenched jaw raised my tearful question to the cosmos: "Why was this taken away?"

"Wrong question," comes back the answer, gentle and clear, in a voice unmistakably Rafe's. "The real question is 'Why was it *given?*'"

It will probably take the rest of my life to work out all the nuances, but the essence of it I saw instantly. It was all right there in that wrenching scene, still raw in my memory, of Prospero and Ariel in their anguished moment of release. I knew even as it flashed by on the stage that this was the chiastic center of whatever painful grace was to be conveyed in this bucking bronco of an Indian-summer romance. Wherever else we were in the playscript—wherever else we were in our *lives*—in this imaginal passage we were to make together we were sacramentally reenacting that great scene.

"In order to find an answer"—had not Helen Luke already announced?—"an individual must seek in the unconscious for his or her own image of an Ariel." Johnny was my Ariel. Into my life he came, that wild, wiry tricksy spirit, plying his joy and his vibrancy like an elemental fountain. Awakening me to the demiurgic force that had gone gray in me for being measured out in teaspoons. Recalling me to the full wingspan of the joy and passion I carried also within myself; my own fierce will to the wildheartedness of life, to the immensity of love, to uncharted seas. To the courage to stand up in my own body, to find the guts and earthiness to speak my own truth, trust my own authority, and do whatever might be required as the world enters these new and difficult times. To this elusive spirit-being, who for a season of life allowed himself to be called "my bird, my chick," I will be forever grateful. In that season I was happier than I have ever been and more beautiful than I will ever be.

The mistake I made was to try to claim this gift in two worlds at once. Enchanted by the magic, I allowed myself to forget that it was only in World 24, by World 24 causality, that any of this would hang together. By the same imaginal light in which I recognized him as Ariel, I recognized as well that there would come a time when he would ask for his freedom back. And if I was slow to return it, preferring to linger in this garden of earthly delights, then the demiurge in him would start to turn dark. He would ask again, this time more urgently, and if I still dragged my feet, he was not about to wait around for the subtle orchestration of the Bard. He would depart from the playscript, rip the staff and book right out of my hands, and if that's what it took, tear the whole stage down to blast his way to freedom.

 la

The mercy is real. But it comes quietly, in the gaps, clad in the vestments of World 12, at first invisible to our eyes.

"You have to endure the tedium till something emerges in it" is how Rafe once put it to me. If you really want to find out what lies behind the mind, the first step is simply to stay present in the absence, not try to fill it with something more familiar, like joy or despair. And yes, at first it feels like death; everything is so deathly monotonous minus that constant roaring and churning you mistake for being alive. But if you push through and watch very closely, something does indeed begin to emerge, bearing the faintest scent of that other intensity.

There was a moment one day, almost artless in its ordinariness, out on Eagle Island, maybe a decade ago. I was simply walking down the road past the old Quinn barn when suddenly I realized, in a moment of complete amazement, that *it*

would all be okay—I could simply dissolve, like a virtual particle, and all would remain serenely undisturbed within the cosmos. Consciousness would do just fine without "me" tending
it. This tiny nanosecond of an independent viewing platform
with all its drama and insistence and earnestness could simply vanish into the whole, and the whole would still be completely *whole*.

"So that's it! What joy!" I said, unconsciously echoing those
immortal words of Ivan Illich at his deathbed breakthrough.[6]
No me, no constructions, no illusions, no pot of gold at the
end of the rainbow, no rainbow even; just an infinite intimacy,
the brilliant blue sky and an old barn, standing like a weather-
beaten sentry in the breeze. Nothing more. Nothing less.
Nothing else.

Huston Smith stands on very much this same precipice in
his remarkable book *Why Religion Matters*, written very close
to the end of his long, wise life. Envisioning his own journey
through the successive layers of dissolving that await him beyond physical death, he writes:

> After I shed my body, I will continue to be conscious of
> the life I have lived and the people who remain on earth.
> Sooner or later, however, there will come a time when no
> one alive will have heard of Huston Smith, let alone have
> known him, whereupon there ceases to be any point in
> my hanging around. Echoing John Chrysostom's re-
> ported farewell, 'Thanks, thanks, for everything; praise,
> praise for it all,' I will then turn my back on planet earth
> and attend to what is more interesting, the beatific vision.
> As long as I continue to be involved with my individual-
> ity, I will retain the awareness that it is I, Huston Smith,
> who is enjoying that vision; and as long as I want to con-
> tinue in that awareness I will be able to do so. For me,

though—mystic by temperament, though here below not by attainment—after oscillating back and forth between enjoying the sunset and enjoying Huston-Smith-enjoy-ing-the-sunset, I expect to find the uncompromised sunset more absorbing. The string will have been cut. The bird will be free.[7]

Prospero and Ariel, doing their archetypal dance one last time . . .

And at that last gateway, all that's left is the gesture itself; even of joy, there is none left to bind. But maybe that gesture is really what it's been about all along, learned over lifetimes, in all worlds, at all densities. Huston's seeing here is so sweet, so wise, so fully tempered. Each stage is recognized. Each world is honored. Nothing is forced or coerced, nothing wrested from one's hands. It's simply given back when ready, like ripe fruit falling from a tree.

 si

Standing where I am now, still barely on the other side of the line gale that parted the seasons of my life, I can already feel the sweetness creeping back in. I feel the goodness of it way more than the loss. The answer was already there, embedded in Rafe's gentle counter question: "Why was it given?" It was *given;* what more really needs to be said? All is given out of love. The cosmos is not treacherous or a trickster, not punitive, but giving and forgiving. It does not set up tests and traps. It does not delight in our failure but gently encourages us onward, to risk and offer everything at even greater depths. "Be patient with all that is unresolved in your heart and try to love the questions themselves," counsels Rilke. I know that I have been given the beginnings of an answer to a lifelong question

I am now barely able to live, and that when I am able to live it in full, then it will be fully revealed. Till then, I know that love still holds and that somewhere there is a world in which all of this will find its place.

I know now as well that there is no conflict between the maps. Permanent individuality or permanent dissolution? They are simply different perspectives, different ways of describing the same infinitely describable reality. From the outer perspective—and it is a good one because that is the place where we actually live and must exercise our human responsibility—the journey looks more like worlds within worlds, cosmic exchange, progressively finer and more adamantine inner bodies leading finally to permanent individuality. This is the journey I have mostly tried to share with you here through these imaginal roadmaps. But the same motion, viewed from the inside, looks more like a steady peeling away of the onion skin, layer upon layer of constructal givens, bound joys, and even finally "*con*-sciousness" itself, the primordial relational ground. They are the same map, viewed under different lights, but each pointing toward that same inscrutable inner unity that some call the absolute and others call the void. Whatever you call it, says Thomas Keating, "It is the safest place in all creation, where gratitude, freedom, and pure love reign supreme."[8]

"When was I ever made less by dying?" asks Rumi. Miraculously, this Prospero mind of mine has now gone strangely silent; it has no opinion on this. I do not need to know into which body, into which subtle form. It is enough to know that I will die into love. Nor will I know exactly what this love looks like on the other side. But when that Ariel moment finally comes, I will know what I have to do. Once again, the scene indelibly seared in my heart, I will stand up, cut the string, and let my beloved tricksy spirit go. And then, in the poverty of my bare self, I will yield myself into the mercy, the true and only second rascooarno.

. . . and yet, tender as I still am in this new place in which I find myself, I wonder how many worlds it will take before I no longer hear that one bird singing terribly afar in the lost lands.

Afterword

A. H. ALMAAS

IN READING THIS book, you have gone through quite a journey of learning and discovery. Cynthia Bourgeault has taken you with her on her own very personal journey of inquiry into the spiritual realms, an inquiry catalyzed by an encounter she had on the earth plane with the man she calls the Greek. Writing this book became her metabolism of this experience as she sought to understand her awakenings and insights within a wider context. Drawing on both her heart and her synthetic intelligence, she has combined elements from many metaphysical maps (Gurdjieff's Ray of Creation, the perennialists' Great Chain of Being, the Sufi planes of being) to create an elaborate new construction. And she has invited you to use this map, if you feel so inclined.

The result is a brilliant synthesis that both situates the imaginal world and gives it more meaning than it has previously had. According to the Sufis, the imaginal world is the in-between world of experience connecting the physical world with the spiritual planes above it. It is where visionary experiences and encounters occur. You find this world in many traditional teachings, not just the Sufi, but it is not always explicitly given a place in the spiritual realm. The Tibetan Buddhist tradition makes use of this world, even though not obvious in its teachings. If you read the biographies of the great masters, like that of Dudjom Lingpa, they are mostly visionary experiences and encounters with deities, bodhisattvas, and dakinis imparting wisdom to the lama. The Sufi biographies mostly describe spiritual illuminations and encounters with previous saints or prophets that are experienced through the inner subtle senses of seeing, hearing, and so on. This is the case, too, in Kabbalah and Christian mysticism.

The author is careful to differentiate the imaginal world from that of human imagination and fantasy. And, she points to the danger of conflating the two, a danger I see happening in many areas. The Sufis see a relationship between human imagination and the imaginal capacity. The imaginal capacity, in perceiving *alam almithal*, utilizes human imagination but takes it to its spiritual possibilities of seeing into the spiritual world. This is similar to using the human intellect when impregnated by the diamonds of the spirit to know spiritual realities and understand them as what they are, free from personal prejudice. Bourgeault goes further than most in her view of the imaginal world; for her it becomes the sphere of spiritual experiencing on any level of subtlety, for it is the nexus to the higher planes of spirit.

I find many gifts here to the reader and to spiritual discourse in our times. It so happens that the Eastern teachings of nonduality have become the lens through which many view spirituality. In my view, this limits spiritual experiencing and the possibilities of the spirit. For in this view, our world, our earthly world, is mostly seen as an illusion or a distorted way of experiencing reality. And that reality is the infinite consciousness or awareness that simply manifests the world as its appearance. Some call the world a convenient fiction. Bourgeault gives the earthly world an importance missing in these nondual teachings, and in this way she is a true representative of the Western spiritual tradition. The Western tradition, as we see in the Sufi planes of being and the four worlds of Kabbalah, gives this world a reality all its own and a significance that is necessary for all planes of being, including that of pure infinite consciousness. It is necessary, for it is the realm that makes sense of why the spirit has in it love, compassion, nobility, beauty, humility, steadfastness, conscience, and so on. Without human beings on earth, where life is full of hardship, it is difficult to see why the divine spirit will need such qualities.

She also emphasizes the place and role of the person, for it is the true person who is the spiritually realized human living on earth. Nondual teachings tend to see the person as the separate ego individuality and cannot conceive of an individual who is not an illusion. This way, they have no way to understand why nondual realization itself is exemplified by human beings, unique persons living a human life, even though inwardly their identity is the vastness of spirit.

Even though her map is admittedly a construction, it is based on experience and is useful for new spiritual illuminations to arise. By the end of the book, she does what most advanced teachings do. Let go of the map, drop the path, and simply be the simplicity.

The construction helps us see how spiritual illumination is an interchange, an exchange, of spiritual substances between different realms. That substance is physical on earth in ordinary experience, but the divine spirit pours as substances of different kinds. That which we call love, compassion, intelligence, will, forgiveness, and so on are substances descending from the higher planes of being to the lower ones. And our own practice, which she puts in the Gurdjieffian language of conscious attention and intentional suffering, generates energies that rise through the imaginal realm to the higher planes of being. It is clear from all of this that all the planes are interconnected; they make up a unity. But a differentiated unity that makes sense of what spiritual progress means.

She also shows, by discussing her ongoing connection to her once-living friend Rafe, that life and experience don't end with physical death. She is not participating here in the naive view of heaven and hell, but of the spiritual world with vistas and life, where her friend Rafe still lives, learns, and ripens since his death a few decades ago. And through her ongoing intimate connection with him, she receives insights that nourish her teaching. In some way, they have become one, an abler soul, and through such unity of inner body, they learn and grow together, birthing a spiritual teaching that illuminates the precious secrets of the Christian revelation. She is on the side of earthly living, and he is on the other side of death. Besides the interesting truth that two human beings can be fused as one soul, she clearly states the view that life continues after death. That depending on our spiritual development on earth, we have different degrees of capacity to live after death. Life continues on the other side, and spiritual progress is even smoother and much more fluid.

Bourgeault also highlights the importance of developing an inner spiritual body. Gurdjieff called it the kesdjan body. This is not simply the vastness of consciousness, as nondualists will tend to think, but an individual body with a true sense of individuality. Not disconnected from the vastness but expressing it, it has a true I, a unique identity, and can develop to further stages of inner body. This is a significant gift to the spiritual seeker: the seeker will not simply dissolve upon enlightenment or death, but with deep spiritual burning can develop a true spiritual inner body. Such a body can develop all the way to the crystalline indestructible body that Gurdjieff has obviously developed since his death. This is actually reminiscent of some of the Buddhist Mahayana teachings. When one reaches a certain stage of illumination, in Buddhism it is called Buddhahood, one's inner subtle body transforms into the vajrakaya, an individual and indestructible spiritual body through which one experiences, acts, and expresses.

The author has breathed life into Gurdjieff's Ray of Creation, illustrating how spiritual illumination progresses in the Western Spiritual Tradition. But she has given all of these gifts by telling her story, personal and vulnerable, human but not only human. We are all this way, human but not only human. We are both human and divine, matter and spirit, with each being true and the two inseparable. In these times, we desperately need to know this, for humanity is facing many challenges. There is much fear, hopelessness, self-centeredness, and anger. And there are dangers in our environment that require the recognition that our physical humanity, even though real and vulnerable, is not separate from an indestructible spiritual essence. The more we intimately know both of our sides, the more effectively and appropriately we can navigate life, death, and after death. And we can also be liberated from much of the suffering by metabolizing it, so that our experience transforms into unity with our inner subtle body of indestructible spirit.

Notes

Prelude: Prospero, Jonah, and "The Greek"

1. Evan Thompson, *Waking, Dreaming, Being* (New York: Columbia University Press, 2015), 359.

2. William Shakespeare, *The Tempest*, act 4, sc. 1.

Chapter One: Introducing the Imaginal

1. It is beyond the scope of this book to give a complete introduction to the Western tradition of perennial wisdom, but an excellent start (beyond an unusually nuanced and helpful introduction on the Wikipedia site) is Aldous Huxley's now classic book *The Perennial Philosophy*, first published in 1945 by Harper and Brothers and in continuous circulation ever since. The perennial philosophy is represented in various flavors and lineages, and while it is impossible to accommodate all the variations under a single philosophical rubric, a good starting point is Huxley's 1944 essay in *Vedanta and the West*, in which he describes "The Minimum Working Hypothesis," the basic outline of the perennial philosophy found in all the mystic branches of the religions of the world:

> That there is a Godhead or Ground, which is the unmanifested principle of all manifestation.
> That the Ground is transcendent and immanent.
> That it is possible for human beings to love, know and, from virtually, to become actually identified with the Ground.
> That to achieve this unitive knowledge, to realize this supreme identity, is the final end and purpose of human existence.
> That there is a Law or Dharma, which must be obeyed, a Tao or Way, which must be followed, if men are to achieve their final end.

2. Valentin Tomberg, *Meditations on the Tarot* (Rockport, MA: Element Books, 1985), 574.

3. You will find these energies described in many places throughout Teilhard's voluminous work, but a good place to begin is with his masterpiece,

The Human Phenomenon, particularly in the Sarah Appleton-Weber translation (Chicago: Sussex Academic Press, 1999), which adds back into the text a crucial diagram in Teilhard's original manuscript (eliminated in later revisions), followed by an extensive and exceedingly helpful commentary in her "Appendix A," 227–32.

4. Lynn Bauman, trans., *The Gospel of Thomas* (logion 77) (Ashland, OR: White Cloud Press, 2002), 163.

5. Jean-Yves Leloup, *The Gospel of Mary Magdalene* (Rochester, VT: Inner Traditions, 2002), 153.

6. Walter Wink, "Easter: What Happened to Jesus?" *Tikkun*, March–April 2008. www.tikkun.org/article_php/MarchAprilTOC2008.

7. For a recent and beautifully displayed version of this map, see Ken Wilber, *Integral Spirituality* (Cambridge, MA: Shambhala Publications, 2007), facing page 27.

Chapter 2: Worlds within Worlds

1. T. S. Eliot, "East Coker," in *The Complete Poems and Plays* (New York: Harcourt, Brace, and World, 1952), 129.

2. These tables are intricately laid out in P. D. Ouspensky's *In Search of the Miraculous* (New York: Harcourt, 1949), still the classic gateway book into the Gurdjieffian universe. See particularly the discussion and diagrams on pages 317–24.

3. Gurdjieff does not technically use the term *imaginal*, but a careful reading of his *Beelzebub's Tales to His Grandson,* particularly in the 1992 edition (Viking Arkana) reveals that he is clearly aware of the distinction between "imagination" (subjective and fanciful) and "imaginal" (in alignment with a direct perception of objective truth emerging from higher realms). His entire chapter "Art" (pages 410–78) traces the disintegration of art as a viaduct for imaginal truth, and his word of choice in the 1992 edition for allegorical literature constructed according to the more ancient objective principle is *imagonisirian* (or, in the 1950 edition, based on a slightly different manuscript version, *similnisian*). For further exploration, see the *Guide and Index to Beelzebub's Tales to His Grandson* (Toronto: Traditional Studies Press, 2003).

4. In the American solfeggio system this note is known as *ti*, but the European models universally (and with much more of a vestigial esoteric memory!) identify this note as *si*.

5. Cynthia Bourgeault, *The Holy Trinity and the Law of Three* (Boulder: Shambhala Publications, 2013), particularly pages 33–36 and all of chapter 4, pages 48–59. The bibliographical references in that book will lead you to the main source material in Ouspensky's *In Search of the Miraculous* and Nicoll's *Psychological Commentaries on the Teachings of Ouspensky and Gurdjieff.* From there the trail branches nearly endlessly.

6. Once again, this is laid out in Ouspensky's *In Search of the Miraculous* (see previous note).

7. Jacob Boehme, *The Way to Christ* (New York: Paulist Press, 1978), 192.

8. Jacob Boehme, *The Clavis or Key and Dialogues on the Supersensual Life* (Kila, MT: Kessinger Publications, 2010), 50.

9. In ascending order, these states of consciousness are known as *gross, subtle, causal,* and *nondual.* For a further explanation, see Ken Wilber, *Integral Spirituality* (Cambridge, MA: Shambhala Publications, 2006), 74; for Wilber's helpful diagram of the interface between stages and states of consciousness, see *Integral Spirituality*, page 88.

10. Pierre Teilhard de Chardin, *The Human Phenomenon*, trans. Sarah Appleton-Weber (Chicago: Sussex Academic Press, 1999), 188.

11. See in particular Bernadette Roberts's *The Real Christ.* Like so much of her later work, this tract is privately published but available for purchase. Googling her name will lead you to the current contact information for a spiral-bound copy of this brilliant and challenging work.

12. The tendency to equate the Christic with the nondual realms (or levels of consciousness) emerges in my estimate out of two conflations, both well intentioned but ultimately unhelpful. The first is the conflation of consciousness and cosmology. While it is certainly beyond question that Jesus as a person modeled the signature traits of what we now call "Christ consciousness," that does not imply that the Christic realm, understood cosmologically, is situated in the nondual bandwidth. The second is the conflation of theology and metaphysics. Because World 3 is the primary ternary and Jesus is classically identified theologically as the second person of the Trinity, Christians are sometimes too quick to assume that this places him—as a human person—in World 3. But the Trinity in World 3 is not yet "Father, Son, and Holy Spirit"; it is the primordial Law of Three. The Trinity as we know it theologically belongs entirely within what I will shortly identify as "the sphere of the personal"—Worlds 12, 24, and 48—where it serves as its central icon and pathway to spiritual fullness. I

will unpack this a bit further in chapter 7, but the fullest exploration is in my book *The Holy Trinity and the Law of Three* (Shambhala Publications, 2013), particularly in section 3.

13. Ladislaus Boros, *The Mystery of Death* (New York: Seabury Press, 1973), 146.

Chapter 3: The Great Exchange

1. William Segal, "The Force of Attention," in *The Structure of Man* (Brattleboro, VT: Green River Press, Stillgate Publishers, 1987), excerpted in *Parabola Magazine*, 15:2.

2. Pierre Teilhard de Chardin, *The Divine Milieu* (New York: Harper Perennial 2001), 111.

3. Cynthia Bourgeault, *The Wisdom Way of Knowing* (San Francisco: Wiley, 2003), 55.

4. As enumerated by St. Paul in Galatians 5:22–23.

5. Lynn Bauman, trans., *The Gospel of Thomas* (logion 108) (Ashland, OR: White Cloud Press, 2002), 225.

6. You will find these sayings quoted in J. G. Bennett, *The Masters of Wisdom* (Wellingborough, Northamptonshire: Turnstone Press, Ltd., 1982), 133–37.

7. Maurice Nicoll, *The New Man* (New York: Penguin Books, 1987), 143.

8. Jacob Boehme, *The Way to Christ* (New York: Paulist Press, 1978), 192.

9. G. I. Gurdjieff, *Beelzebub's Tales to His Grandson* (New York: Viking Arcana, 1992), 351.

Chapter 4: Imaginal Causality

1. For an interesting recent read in this regard, see Carlo Rovelli, *The Order of Time* (New York: Riverhead Books, 2018).

2. Pierre Teilhard de Chardin, *The Human Phenomenon*, trans. Sarah Appleton-Weber (Chicago: Sussex Academic Press, 1999), 3.

3. Lynn Bauman, trans., *The Gospel of Thomas* (logion 22) (Ashland, OR: White Cloud Press, 2002), 51–52.

4. Bruno Barnhart, *The Good Wine: Reading John from the Center* (New York/ Mahwah NJ: Paulist Press, 1993).

5. Barnhart, *The Good Wine*, 240.

6. I believe, incidentally, that exactly this same chiastic mandala—Jesus as the Lord of the New Creation—is strongly at play in Teilhard de Chardin's work and in fact furnishes the key to a chiastic reconstruction of his collected works. While I won't load the decks with that in this book, it might furnish an intriguing new starting point for a desideratum yet to be achieved in Teilhardian scholarly circles: a comprehensive reorganizing of his canon in a way that makes it both more accessible and more internally coherent.

7. The imaginal overlay here is actually a bit more intricate. This scriptural text is not merely chosen out of thin air; it is the exact text that decades earlier, hearing it at the same dinner table, had caused the young general in a fit of cynicism and despair to break off his budding romance and depart abruptly to pursue his worldly fortunes along other byways. The very words that had once symbolized the decimation of his hopes now convey their final restitution.

8. Thomas Merton, "Hagia Sophia," in *A Thomas Merton Reader*, ed. Thomas P. McDonnell (New York: Doubleday/Image Books, 1974), 509.

9. Merton, "Special Closing Prayer," in *Thomas Merton Reader*, 512. Offered at the First Spiritual Summit Conference in Calcutta by Thomas Merton, December 1968.

10. This point is subtly reinforced in the structure of the chiasm itself. On the left side, where time still flows forward according to linear causality, all is heartbreak and loss. On the right side, where time gushes forth ("backward") out of the imaginal Jacob's well, all is plenitude and grace. The scenes, the images, and, in two cases, even the text ("Mercy and faithfulness have met"; "Oh, how you will enchant the angels!") are perfectly symmetrically balanced.

11. Cynthia Bourgeault, *Mystical Hope* (Cambridge, MA: Cowley Publications, 2001), 65.

Chapter 5: The Art of Shapeshifting

1. Charles Baudelaire, "Correspondances," in *The Flowers of Evil/Les Fleurs du Mal*, trans. William Aggeler (Fresno, CA: Academy Library Guild, 1954).

2. Jacques Lusseyran, *And There Was Light* (New York: Parabola Books, 1998), 95.

3. T. S. Eliot, "The Dry Salvages," in *The Complete Poems and Plays* (New York: Harcourt, Brace, and World, 1952), 136.

4. Thomas Kelly, *A Testament of Devotion* (New York: HarperCollins, 1992), 5.

Chapter 6: Imaginal Purification

1. Ken Wilber used these terms in his earlier maps of the levels of consciousness but later abandoned them—not, however, before passing on the original roadmap to Jim Marion, whose influential book *Putting on the Mind of Christ* (Charlottesville, VA: Hampton Roads, 2000) made extensive and helpful use of these categories.

2. For a further elucidation of this horrifying typology, see *Beelzebub's Tales* (Viking Arcana edition), 369–73.

3. This descriptor comes from Ken Wilber, as part of his helpful exploration of the role of the personal and relational in the life of higher consciousness. See Ken Wilber, *Integral Spirituality* (Cambridge: Shambhala Publications, 2007), 158–61.

4. This is not a direct quotation but rather my paraphrase of a very closely argued section of an impassioned and sophisticated argument offered by this anonymous fourteenth-century English monk in an essay now most widely known as "A Letter of Spiritual Direction" in *The Pursuit of Wisdom*, translated and edited by James A. Walsh (New York: Paulist Press, 1988). See, in particular, on page 226: "There is no need, no order to increase your perfection, to go back and feed your faculties by contemplating the qualities of your being . . . [but simply by] offering up to God that simple awareness of the substance of your being."

5. Cynthia Bourgeault, *The Heart of Centering Prayer: Nondual Christianity in Theory and Practice* (Boulder: Shambhala Publications, 2016).

6. Beatrice Bruteau, "Prayer and Identity," quoted in Thomas Keating and others, *Spirituality, Contemplation, and Transformation* (New York: Lantern Books, 2008), 101.

7. Kabir Helminski, *Living Presence: A Sufi Way to Mindfulness and the Essential Self* (New York: Jeremy Tarcher/Putnam, 1992), 157.

8. Symeon the New Theologian, "Three Methods of Attention and Prayer," in *Writings from the Philokalia: On Prayer of the Heart*, trans. E. Kadloubovsky and G. E. H. Palmer (London: Faber and Faber, 1992), 158.

9. Symeon, "Three Methods." For more on Symeon, the practice of

nonattachment, and the striking parallels between his teachings on attention of the heart and classic Asian notions of nonduality, see chapter 5, "Further to Symeon the New Theologian," in my book *The Heart of Centering Prayer: Nondual Christianity in Theory and Practice.*

10. Maurice Nicoll, *Psychological Commentaries on the Teachings of Ouspensky and Gurdjieff* vol. 5, (Boston: Shambhala Publications, 1984), 1,542.

11. Quoted from Thomas Kelly, *A Testament of Devotion* (New York: Harper-Collins, 1992), 26.

12. Jacob Boehme, *The Way to Christ* (New York: Paulist Press, 1978), 123–24.

13. I realize that I may be opening a can of worms here and need to further clarify what I have stated in the text. I believe that evil is absolutely real, and as I have already suggested in my reflection on the hell realms (Trope to Chapter 3), that it can and does take root in the innocent soil of our human hurt and pain. But full demonic stature is essentially a "C-influence" phenomenon—only on the opposite side of the moral spectrum (see page 114 for a description of C influences); fortunately, such emergences are rare. As I have already mentioned earlier in chapter 6 (page 106), Gurdjieff coined the term *hasnamuss* to describe beings in which a natural proclivity to evil is combined with a supremely powerful and disciplined personal will. These people can and do inflict considerable damage, not only on our planet and its inhabitants but upon the image of humanity itself. But even in these situations, the very restlessness and distractibility of the human condition makes it difficult for the demonic (or anything else, for that matter) to take permanent root. What Teilhard calls *tatonnement*—the constant play of trial and error that governs our erratic evolutionary trajectory here—is also, blessedly, a shield against being permanently trapped in these grotesquely distorted psychic constellations. The energy by which we cavitate is also the force by which we rebound—one of the cosmic safeguards apparently and providentially woven into the boundary conventions of World 48.

Chapter 7: What Are We Here for?

1. William Segal, "The Force of Attention," *The Structure of Man* (Brattleboro, VT: Green River Press, Stillgate Publishers, 1987), excerpted in *Parabola Magazine*, 15:2, 332–33.

2. The term *axial religion* was first coined by the German philosopher Karl Jaspers, who called the age "axial" because it laid the spiritual and moral

foundations on which religious consciousness still essentially rests. Karl Jaspers, *The Origin and Goal of History*, trans. Michael Bullock (New Haven: Yale University Press, 1923). While his paradigm has been extremely influential, it is not without its critics. For a brief but helpful summary of the ongoing discussion, see Ilia Delio, *Christ in Evolution* (Maryknoll, NY: Orbis Books, 2008), 185 n31.

3. Teilhard de Chardin, *The Human Phenomenon*, trans. Sarah Appleton-Weber (Chicago: Sussex Academic Press, 1999), 211.

4. Helen Luke, *Old Age* (New York: Parabola Books, 1987), 95.

5. Jacob Boehme, *The Clavis or Key and Dialogues on the Supersensual Life* (Kila, MT: Kessinger Publishing, 2010), 15–16.

6. For my own deeper exploration on how Teilhard works with love as a cosmogonic principle, see Bourgeault, "Love Is the Answer, What Is the Question?" in a short volume of my selected writings by that same name (Northeast Wisdom, 2018), 1–6.

7. For this more extensive exploration of the spirituality of kenosis, see in particular my *Centering Prayer and Inner Awakening* (Cambridge MA: Cowley Publications, 2004), 83–88; *The Wisdom Jesus* (Boston: Shambhala Publications, 2008), 62–74; *The Heart of Centering Prayer* (Boulder: Shambhala Publications, 2016), 32–36, 68–76.

8. It is a wonder to hear Jesus's third beatitude with fresh ears in this translation: "Blessed are the apprivoisé (rather than "the meek"): for they shall inherit the earth."

9. Teilhard de Chardin, *The Human Phenomenon*, 65.

10. This statement may at first strike you as strange, since World 96 as we have been describing it here is characterized by insentience, rigidity, and increasing mechanicality. But from Gurdjieff's perspective, World 96 is also *re*, the moon, which is under active development—in fact, the most actively developing region of the Megalocosmos, drawing its life from the biosphere by means of the very mechanicality and insentience that is death in the human realm.

11. The relationship between essence and personality is actually a bit more complicated than I have initially presented it here; some of this complication is contributed by Gurdjieff himself. As Roger Lipsey helpfully clarifies (in a private correspondence, February 24, 2019), "In Gurdjieff's teachings there are two values, far from identical, for the word Essence.

The first value is in Ouspensky's *Fragments*, [*In Search of the Miraculous*] where G. draws the distinction between essence and personality and emphasizes that essence in an adult can be like that of a five- or six-year-old, undeveloped. It is our best potential, it is what we really are or can be—but it is undeveloped in many people. In *Beelzebub's Tales*, the value is completely different: the 'Essence-loving Ashiata Shiemash' provides the best example, but there are many. Essence there refers to the fully developed capacity for faith, love, hope, conscience, with the implication that Essence is aware of the larger whole, the cosmic whole, to which it belongs: membership at least of world 24 if not also 12."

In my own explication, I am obviously drawing more fully on the first value, but with due recognition of that oft-quoted Gurdjieffian aphorism, "Behind personality stands essence, behind essence stands 'Real I', and behind 'Real I' stands God." The danger in this aphorism, however, is that which makes the whole relationship a bit pat, with "Real I" appearing to be merely the next stage in a linear progression, which it manifestly is not.

My own tentative solution to this conundrum might be to relate essence and "Real I" by means of the Law of Three, in full recognition of an underlying Trogoautoegocratic process in which both upward and downward transmission also have their values. If essence functions as first force, finitude as second force (in the way we have been discussing in this chapter), and conscious work as third, then "Real I" emerges—always as an imaginal substantiality—as the new arising from their interwoven dynamism. It is a progression, but not a linear one, for it manifests under a nonlinear causality. From the perspective of the Trogoautoegocrat, "Real I" is what emerges when essence—which "comes from the stars," as Gurdjieff liked to say—is cured and tempered in the refiners's fire of finitude and handed upward as "food" for the higher realms.

The catch, of course, is that in the usual state of human affairs essence is passive, dominated by the agendas and drama of the personality. As personality becomes "food" for essence, essence is correlatively empowered to become the real master of the inner household. It enters the playing field as a genuine player, and the work of inner transformation begins in earnest.

Chapter 8: The Conscious Circle of Humanity

1. Some of you, I suspect, may be worrying at this point that I am merely "channeling" Rafe, allowing his presence (or my reconstructed memory of that presence) to overpower my own will and voice. This is not at all the

case, and I discuss this point at some length in my first book, *Love Is Stronger Than Death*, particularly in chapters 12 and 13 ("Rafe After Death" and "Do the Dead Grow?"). There I explore my totally surprising discovery that the same fluid give-and-take that marked our conversations during our human time together carries over fully into this new configuration. Conscious love remains conscious love, no matter what world it is practiced in.

2. The closer analogue within a Christian frame of reference would be the Communion of Saints, if the term is understood in the traditional way as referring not simply to every baptized Christian, but rather, only to those specially attained ones to whom one prays by name for assistance and encouragement.

3. Ilia Delio, *Making All Things New* (Maryknoll, NY: Orbis Books, 2015), 135.

4. Pierre Teilhard de Chardin, *The Divine Milieu* (New York: Harper Perennial, 2001), 110.

5. Helen Luke, *Old Age* (New York: Parabola Books, 1987), 79, 83.

6. G. I. Gurdjieff, *Beelzebub's Tales to His Grandson* (New York: Viking Arkana, 1992), 324.

7. This story is recorded in Matthew 4:1–11, Mark 1:12–13, and Luke 4:1–12.

8. Pierre Teilhard de Chardin, *The Heart of Matter*, trans. René Hague (New York: Harcourt, 1978), 102.

9. Larry Collins and Dominique Lapierre, *Is Paris Burning?* (New York, Penguin Books, 1965).

Chapter 9: Second Body, Abler Soul

1. This is another fascinating shade of meaning added to that already venerable spiritual teaching, "Die before you die."

2. Beatrice Bruteau, "Prayer and Identity," in Thomas Keating et al. *Spirituality, Contemplation, and Transformation: Writings on Centering Prayer* (New York: Lantern Books, 2008), p. 111.

3. Maurice Nicoll, *Psychological Commentaries on the Teachings of Ouspensky and Gurdjieff*, Volume 3 (Boulder, CO: Shambhala Publications, 1984), 927.

4. Valentin Tomberg, *Anthroposophical Studies in the New Testament* (Spring Valley, NY; Candeur Manuscripts, 1985), 135.

5. Jacob Boehme, *Forty Questions of the Soul*, 256.

6. Boris Mouravieff, *Gnosis* (Newbury, MA: Praxis Institute Press, 1989).

7. *A Recapitulation of the Lord's Prayer* (anonymous, privately circulated publication, 88–89). The author was an English gentleman and student of P. D. Ouspensky, who, along with a small group of Ouspensky's most committed disciples, was with Ouspensky at the time of his death. So moved was he by this death that he withdrew into solitude in India for more than a decade. This small, privately circulated volume represents the synthesis of his lifelong erudition and spiritual wisdom.

Chapter 10: The Second Rascooarno

1. Helen Luke, *Old Age* (New York: Parabola Books, 1987), 36.

2. William Shakespeare, *The Tempest* (Epilogue).

3. William Shakespeare, *The Tempest* (act 5, sc. 2).

4. With these words—"magnetical hunger"—I am intentionally alluding to Jacob Boehme, who uses the phrase to describe the first painful self-tensioning of the divine will into an insatiable craving (insatiable because there is as yet nothing through which it can slake itself), which establishes the initial current in the heretofore bottomless stillness of the divine will. Through this current (the headwaters of the primordial eros), all things will come into being. See my earlier discussion of Boehme in Chapter 7, (page 130) with regard to the origin of World 3.

5. e. e. cummings, *Complete Poems 1904–1962*, ed. George J. Firmage (New York: Liveright Publishing, 1994), 146.

6. Leo Tolstoy, *The Death of Ivan Illich*, trans. Richard Pevear and Larissa Volokhonsky (New York: Vintage Books, 2009), 53.

7. Huston Smith, *Why Religion Matters* (San Francisco: HarperSanFrancisco, 2001), 290–91.

8. Thomas Keating, *Reflections on the Unknowable* (New York: Lantern Books, 2014), 150.

Index

Page numbers in italics refer to diagrams.

abler souls, 2–3, 21–22, 166–69, 179
Ali, Hameed, 162
apprivoiser, 132, 134, 167, 202n8
Atlantis, 142, 151
attention, 54, 106, 109–10, 115, 123, 127, 153, 160–61
radial energy and, 17, 41, 51, 59
axial religion, 124–25, 143, 201–2n2
second age of, 144, 152, 155, 169–71

Babette's Feast (Dinesen), 76–80, *82–83*, 89, 95, 144, 147–48, 156, 199n7, 199n10
Babylon, 142, 143, 152, 155
Barnhart, Bruno, 71–73, *74*, 90–91, 99, 101, 170
Baudelaire, Charles, 68, 86, 89
Beethoven, Ludwig van, 126–27
Benedictine monasticism, 99–103, 173–78
Bennett, J. G., 34, 166–67
Bible, 20, 100–102, 114, 143, 155
Genesis, 72–73, *74*
Gospel of John, 34, 71–73, *74*, 90–91, 101, 125
Gospel of Luke, 69–71, *70*, 147
Gospel of Matthew, 157–58
Gospel of Thomas, 18, 43–44, 68, 145, 162
Jonah in, 8–11, 21, 102
Psalm 85, 78, 199n7

signs in, 69, 86, 87, 149, 150
St. Paul, 15, 16, 102, 109, 120, 131
See also Jesus
Blake, William, 184
bodies, 124–25, 164
Boehme, Jacob, 25, 32–33, 55, 115, 129, 158, 163, 205n4
on majesty, 5, 165
Book of Common Prayer, Episcopal, 183
Boros, Ladislaus, 39
Bourgeault, Cynthia
previous books by, 3, 27, 50–51, 66, 80, 108, 202n6, 204n1
relationships of (*see* Kontsas, Johnny "The Greek"; Robin, Raphael "Rafe")
teachers of, 25, 71, 101, 115, 170, 173–78
Boyle, Joseph, 170, 173–78
Bruteau, Beatrice, 108, 158, 170

causality, imaginal, 11, 19–22, 65–122
in Benedictine monasticism, 99–103
as chiastic (*see* chiasm)
consistency required for, 111–13, 120
distorted interpretation of, 105–8, 121
force of, 19–22, 86, 91–94
guidelines for, 119–22
heart and, 108–11, 113, 114, 122
obedience to, 113–15

as patterned, 68–69, 75–76,
    86–87, 120
as surprising, 95–97, 121
symbolism of, 68, 86–89, 99–100,
    105–6, 109, 120, 153
time and, 86, 89–91, 99, 120
chiasm, 68–81, *82–83*, 85–86, 89–91,
    101, 132–35, 188, 199n10
diagrams of, *70, 74, 83, 133*
Choltitz, Dietrich von, 156
Christianity, 113–14, 124–25, 170
    Inner tradition in, 81, 108, 152,
        154, 157, 163
    Mysteries of, 52–53, 129, 135
    See also Bible; Jesus
Cloud of Unknowing, The, 108
conscious circle, 139–57, 165, 176–
    78, 204n2
    charter of, 3, 60, 131, 140, 145
    cosmic dialysis by, 64, 145–49,
        160
    guidance from, 145, 149–53
    participants in, 157–69
    as third force, 145, 153–55
    Wisdom schools and, 103, 142–
        44, 150–53, 154–55, 170
    See also Robin, Raphael "Rafe":
        relationship after death
consciousness, 33, 192
    collective shifts in, 143–44, 150–
        53, 154–55, 169–71
    individual shifts in, 43–47, 53–
        58, 93–94
    levels of, 21, 30–41, 106–8,
        197n9, 200n1, 200n3
constructions, illusions vs., 1, 3–4,
    12, 20, 180, 182–83
Corbin, Henry, 19, 20
cosmic equilibrium, 24, 124, 126,
    132, 141
    destabilization of, 45, 116, 144
    entropy vs., 24, 48, 51, 54, 59, 123
cummings, e. e., 187

death
    second body and, 157–69, 204n1
    second rascooarno and, 164–65,
        169, 177, 179–82, 189–93
    of spiritual masters, 170–78
    See also conscious circle
Death of Ivan Illich (Tolstoy), 190
de Pasquale String Quartet, 126–27,
    131
de Ruiter, John, 115
Dialogue of the Carmelites (Poulenc),
    176

Earth. *See* World 48 (earth realm)
Eckhart, Meister, 113
Egypt, 142, 143, 155
Eliot, T. S., 23, 91
Ellis, Peter, 71–72
energy, 17, 48, 91–92
    radial, 18, 39, 46, *49*, 49, 51, 59,
        93, 145, 152, 161
    toxic, 44, 94, 106–7, 111, 146, 162
Eucharist, 52–53
evil, 63, 106–7, 115–16, 201n13
evolution, 28, 43–47, 143–44, 150–
    53, 154–55, 169–71
exchange, imaginal, 23–25, 39, 41,
    43–61, 123–78
    love and, 129–35, *133*, 202n6
    mechanics of, 47–51
    as reciprocal feeding, 24–25,
        47, 125–26, 140, 166
    with the dead, 139–57, 165,
        176–78

faith, 16, 49–50, 120

God, 26, 32–33, 89, 123–35, 195n1
    Christ and, 39, 102, 125, 131
    heart of, 14, 107, 128–30
    suffering of, 55–56, 60, 124, 175
grace, 96–97

Great Chain of Being. *See* Ray of Creation

Gurdjieff, G. I., 2, 5, 24–41, 46, 112, 155–56, 159, 174

    on A, B, and C influences, 114–16, 162, 201n13

    Beelzebub's Tales to His Grandson by, 142–43, 150–51, 163, 196n3, 203n11

    on conscious circle, 3, 60, 139–40, 155–56

    on conscious labor and intentional suffering, 54–58, 160, 167

    on ecological catastrophe, 25, 45

    on evil, 106, 201n13

    on Fourth Way, 60, 167

    on Law of Three, 33, 38–39, 135, 153, 177, 203n11

    on Laws of Accident and Fate, 115–16, 153

    on objective, 94, 148

    on second rascooarno, 181

    on Ray of Creation, 24, 26–30, *29, 31*, 116

    on reciprocal feeding, 24–25, 47, 125–26, 140, 166

    on self, 108, 136–37, 202–3n11

    on soul, 57–58, 60, 161, 163, 165

    on third force, 95–96

    on Trogoautoegocrat, 24, 43–44, 52, 57, 125–26, 132, 144, 203n11

    on Wisdom schools, 142–43, 150–51, 152

    on worlds, 14, 30, 32–41, *40*, 47–49, 96, 115–16, 119, 202n10

hell. *See* World 192

Helminski, Kabir, 108–9

Holy Isle, 148–49

imaginal, 13–22, 81, 119–22, 183

    assistance (*see* conscious circle)

    causality (*see* causality, imaginal)

    exchange (*see* exchange, imaginal)

    heart and, 13–15, 108–11, 113, 130, 151, 200–201n9

    imaginary vs., 15–16, 19, 121, 196n3

    laws governing, 48–49, *49*

    mechanics, 47–51

    purification, 105–17

    as realm, 14–17, 28, 32, 36, 38–39

    self (*see* second body)

    See also World 24

Islam, 128, 154

Jaspers, Karl, 201–2n2

Jesus, 39, 125, 131, 150

    Ascension of, 20, 93

    beatitudes of, 108, 202n8

    Christ Consciousness and, 35, 109, 131, 197n12

    Eucharist and, 52–53

    Gospel of John on, 71–73, *74*, 75, 90–91, 199n6

    lectio divina and, 101–2

    on realms, 14, 36, 43–44, 56, 96

    Zacchaeus and, 70–71, *70*

Jones, Alan, 115

Judaism, 139, 143, 155

Jung, C. G., 87, 101

Keating, Thomas, 101–2, 113, 192

    death of, 170, 173–78

Kelly, Thomas, 97

kesdjan body. *See* second body

Kingdom of Heaven, 36, 53, 136

Kontsas, Johnny "The Greek," 6–12, 21, 34, 63–64, 88, 91, 94, 116–17, 169, 182, 184–85, 187–89

lectio divina, 100–102

Leloup, Jean-Yves, 93

Little Prince (Saint-Exupéry), 132, 134
Losal, Lama Yeshe, 149, 155
love, 80, 120, 125, 147, 156, 175
  conscious, 166–69
  as fruit of spirit, 53, 59, 146
  lack of, 107
  realms and, 34, 35, 39, 64
  role of in cosmos, 129–35, *133*, 191–92, 202n6
Luke, Helen, 128–29, 135, 147
  on *The Tempest*, 180–81, 184, 186, 188
Lusseyran, Jacques, 88–89

Merton, Thomas, 79–80
mi-fa junction point, 27–28, 46, 51, 54, 57, 59, 75, 122, 129, 136, 141
mindfulness, 54, 56
Moore, James, 27
morality, 44–46, 106–7, 149
Mouravieff, Boris, 167
musical scale, 26–27, 196n4

Nicoll, Maurice, 54, 61, 160
nonduality, 35, 136, 173, 197n9, 197n12, 200–201n9
  in imaginal realm, 48, *49*
  in second axial age, 152, 170

Ouspensky, P. D., 32, 61, 203n11, 205n7
Out of Africa (Dinesen), 18

Panikkar, Raimon, 170
perennial wisdom, 15, 26, 147, 195n1
personal, sphere of, 132–35, *133*, 164, 197n12
personality, 37, 136–37, 202–3n11
perspective, 66–67, 89, 108
Popper, Karl, 11
psychic force. *See* energy

quantum physics, 66, 92–93, 135, 144, 145, 147

Ray of Creation, 24, 26–30, *29*, *31*, 124, 140–41
  in chiastic form, 132–35, *133*
  as Great Chain of Being, 17, 35, 116, 125, 128
  realms, 14–15, 23–41, *29*, *31*, *40*, 115–16, 132–35, *134*, 192
  heirarchy of, 124–25, 129
  See also imaginal; *specific Worlds*
Rilke, Rainer Maria, 191
Roberts, Bernadette, 35, 170
Robin, Raphael "Rafe," 1–6, 170
  relationship after death, 2–6, 9–12, 65, 80, 116–17, 121, 140, 159, 167–69, 179, 188, 191, 203–4n1
  relationship before death, 1–2, 92, 111, 112, 114, 174
  spiritual study engaged by, 54, 60–61, 139–40, 150, 159–60
  wisdom from, 1, 93, 119, 147, 189
Rumi, 168, 179, 192

Saint Benedict, 99, 102, 113
saints, 21–22, 91, 159, 161–62, 204n2
second body, 48–49, 52, 60, 87, 157–69, 204n1
  building of, 115, 159–60
  death and, 157–69, 181, 189–93, 204n1
  force of, 160–62
  individuality of, 58, 141, 158–59, 163–66, 169, 192
  "Real I" and, 108, 137, 158, 164, 203n11
  shared with beloved, 166–69, 179
Segal, William, 44, 51, 59, 123, 161

self, egoic vs. witnessing, 107–11,
   122, 135–38, 152, 189–93
Shiemash, Ashiata, 142, 150, 151,
   203n11
Smith, Huston, 190–91
Sona, Ajahn, 152
Soul. *See* second body
spiritual practice, 53–57, 105–17,
   136, 150, 160, 189
   fruits of, 46, 49, 53, 59, 146
   specific, 99–103, 110, 147
Sufism, 105, 114, 154, 161–62
   death in, 59, 204n1
   Gurdjieff and, 25, 54, 196n3
   imaginal in, 15, 16, 19, 87, 94,
      108–9
Symeon the New Theologian, 109–
   10, 200–201n9
synchronicity, *49*, 68, 75, 89–90, 120

Taizé chant, 148
Teilhard de Chardin, Pierre, 5, 25,
   30, 35, 145, 153, 199n6, 201n13
   on counterentropic, 18, 41
   on energy, 18, 39, 49, 195–96n3
   on evolution, 28, 150, 151–53,
      169
   on faith, 49–50
   on God, 107, 125
   on love, 34, 202n6
   on noosphere, 36, 46, 146, 152
   on personal, 59, 134
   on perspective, 67, 86
Tempest, The (Shakespeare), 6, 12,
   180–93 passim
Thompson, Evan, 1
Tibetan Buddhism, 147, 149, 155,
   176–77
time, *49*, 66, 75–76, 86, 89–91, 99,
   120
Tomberg, Valentin, 17, 34, 39,
   113–14, 160
Trinity, 33, 197n12

truth, 1, 3–4, 12, 20, 153, 180,
   182–83

Wilber, Ken, 21, 94, 106, 200n1,
   200n3
Wink, Walter, 19–20, 50, 93
Wisdom schools, 103, 142–44, 150–
   53, 154–55, 170
World 1 (Godhead), 32–33, 56, 135
World 3 (primordial ternary), 33,
   135, 153, 197n12, 205n4
World 6 (causal), 34, 35, 55, 106,
   141–42, 164, 174, 177
   eros and, 34, 39, 79, 130, 135,
      166–67
World 12 (Christic), 35–36, 52–53,
   55, 132, 164, 165, 167, 174, 189
   in *Babette's Feast*, 76, 79
   in Law of Three, 38–39, 177
World 24 (Kingdom of Heaven),
   36, 85, 109, 121, 152, 177, 189,
   202–3n11
   imaginal as, 38–39, 47
   Eucharist and, 52–53, 132
   misuse of, 106–7, 262
   laws governing, 47–49, *49*, 113,
      145
   self in, 107–8, 111, 135
   See also imaginal; *mi-fa* junction
      point; World 48 (earth realm):
      World 24 within
World 48 (earth realm), 23, 27, 30,
   32, 36–37, 38–39, 119, 183–84
   ecological crisis in, 25, 45, 144,
      170
   Eucharist and, 52–53
   laws governing, 14–15, 47–49, *49*,
      101, 128, 201n13
   purpose of, 123–38, 163
   support for (*see* conscious circle)
   toxicity of, 44, 59, 146–47
   World 24 within, 50, 53–61, 65,
      89, 91, 96, 128, 131, 136

World 96 (formatory), 37, 54, 55, 57,
    63, 119, 135, 141, 202n10
World 192 (hell realms), 37–38, 55,
    63–64, 135, 146, 201n13
    Christian conceptions of, 14, 26,
        44–45, 143
World War II, 148, 155–56

Yagan, Murat, 154, 161, 170

Zacchaeus, 69–71, *70*, 115

About the Author

A modern-day mystic, Episcopal priest, theologian, and retreat leader, Cynthia Bourgeault divides her time between solitude at her seaside hermitage in Maine and a demanding schedule traveling globally to promote the rediscovery of the Christian contemplative path. She has been a long-time advocate of Centering Prayer and has worked closely with the community of teachers of that practice, including Thomas Keating, Bruno Barnhart, and Richard Rohr. She is a founding director of both the Contemplative Society and the Aspen Wisdom School, and she continues to contribute to the Contemplative Society in her role as principal teacher and advisor. She was the recipient of the 2014 Contemplative Voices award from Shalem Institute. Cynthia's articles and essays have appeared in many journals and publications, and she is the author of numerous books, including *The Wisdom Jesus*, *The Meaning of Mary Magdalene*, *The Holy Trinity and the Law of Three*, and *The Heart of Centering Prayer*.